POST-MIGRATION ETHNICITY

Post-migration ethnicity

De-essentializing cohesion, commitments and comparison

edited by
Gerd Baumann
and Thijl Sunier

Distribution outside The Netherlands
MARTINUS NIJHOFF International
2501 AX The Hague
The Netherlands

CIP-DATA KONINKLIJKE BIBLIOTHEEK, DEN HAAG

Post-migration
Post-migration ethnicity. De-essentializing cohesion, commitments, and comparison /
Gerd Baumann and Thijl Sunier (eds.) - Amsterdam : Het Spinhuis. - With ref.
ISBN 90-5589-020-0
Subject headings: anthropology / ethnicity.

Typesetting by Hanneke Kossen
Cover design by Jos Hendrix
Printed and bound in the Netherlands

HET SPINHUIS Publishers
Oudezijds Achterburgwal 185, 1012 DK Amsterdam, The Netherlands

Contents

III Comparison: not ethnic cultures but collective contingencies

Introduction
De-essentializing ethnicity

Gerd Baumann and Thijl Sunier

'We need to recognize that [...] dichotomized cultural differences [...] are vastly overstated in ethnic discourse,' said Fredrik Barth (1994a: 30) in opening the Amsterdam conference at which the contributions here assembled were first discussed. In re-writing their papers for publication, the contributors took heed of this timely caution, and they were further made aware of two other sign-posts, sent out to them in the editorial process: one copy of the Comaroffs' (1992) refutation of primordialist approaches to ethnicity, and one of Max Weber's ([1912], 1978) much-neglected disavowal of 'ethnicity' as an analytical category. For editors to tempt contributors into re-reading, rather than re-writing to meet a deadline, may be an unusual strategy; to send them a text that is 75 years old must appear slightly eccentric. Yet there was a topical reason to fall back on Weber in treating of ethnicity in the mid-1990s. There is a recent consensus on de-essentializing our approaches to ethnicity; yet the more we follow this path, the more we may end up with Weber's dismissal of our analytic topic itself. 'All in all', concluded Weber,

> 'the notion of "ethnically" determined social action subsumes phenomena that a rigorous sociological analysis [...] would have to distinguish carefully. [...] It is certain that in this process [of examination] the collective term "ethnic" would be abandoned, for it is unsuitable for a really rigorous analysis.' (Weber 1978, 395)

The statement is shocking, not only for its uncharacteristic boldness, but also for what it may have to say about, or in this case to, a group of anthropologists writing about 'Post-Migration Ethnicity'. Was Weber completely misguided in his prophecy, or has something gone fundamentally wrong with the way in which we, and our contemporaries, have come to view ethnicity?

Weber, we concluded, might still be proven right; but one mighty factor has come to intervene in the course of the 75 years since his writing. Ideas about matters called 'ethnic' are no longer the preserve of social scientists alone, but have conquered a strategic space in the language and the self-understandings of millions of people in the wake of international migration. It is as easy, in 1995, to hear the word 'ethnic' from a Turkish informant in the Netherlands, as from a Dutch anthropologist who writes about him or her. The word 'ethnic', like the word 'culture', has left the confines of the academe and celebrates a new life, or rather new lives, in the streets of 'immigrant quarters', in the pages of newspapers 'ethnic' or 'mainstream', and in the discourse of politicians and news presenters, artists and even marketing experts. With the latter, things 'ethnic' sell as a style; with most of the others, they sell as a problem. 'Ethnic' distinctions have become the bugbear of labour markets and housing statistics, educational achievement and cultural or multi-cultural provision. Their persistence and social efficacy have even shaken the modernist faith in free and universal social mobility and undermined all manner of received ideas about the 'nation'-state (van der Veer in press). There is a deeply ironic twist in these developments. Whilst Weber threw doubt on the value of 'ethnicity' for a rational social analysis, the very social facts so labelled have come to throw doubt on the Weberian vision of an increasing rationalization of political thought, economic systems, and cultural practice. Faced with this reversal, Weber might well endorse the Comaroffs' analysis of what has happened in post-migration ethnicity:

> '[I]n systems where "ascribed" cultural differences rationalize structures of inequality, ethnicity takes on a cogent existential reality. It is this process of reification [...] that gives it the appearance of being an autonomous factor in the ordering of the social world.' (Comaroff and Comaroff 1992, 61)

'Ethnic' difference has indeed been subjected to a large-scale process of reification as Berger and Luckmann (1967) theorized it with such classic lucidity:

'Reification is the apprehension of human phenomena as if they were things, that is, [...] the apprehension of the products of human activity *as if* they were something other than human products – such as facts of nature [...]. Man, the producer of a world, is apprehended as its product, and human activity as an epiphenomenon of non-human processes' (Berger and Luckmann 1967, 106).

'Ethnicity' has been styled into a 'fact of life' in that consciously multi-culturalist dimension of post-migration culture which most metropolitan countries have come to share. It is no longer a value-free 'fact' that should figure in public statistics, but a fact of 'life' that appeals to sup-posedly 'natural' distinctions, such as ethnos or descent, to explain 'cultural' differences. That such reification, or misplaced concreteness, can make no sense to the analyst of social life, is nothing new: 'Even while apprehending the world in reified terms, man continues to pro-duce it' (Berger and Luckmann 1967, 107). The question, though, which Weber did not have to face, is how the analyst should treat 'ethnicity' when the concept itself has become a factor in social life. We can no longer discard it as an analytically impotent term and be done with it. Yet nor can we rehabilitate it as a self-evident, quasi biological explanation of what, as social scientists, we see around us and wish to understand.

The solution to this conondrum is, at present, to be found mainly in programmes. It is wrong, so the latest consensus has found, to essen-tialize ethnicity or, for that matter, culture. The new de-essentializing consensus can be found in writings so diverse as Al-Azmeh (1994) and Barth (1994b), Keesing (1994) and Sahlins (1994), Turner (1993) and Vayda (1994). Even the Boasian heritage of many American anthropol-ogists, which views culture as the collective property of an ethnos, has been unable to stem the new anti-essentialist programme. Yet program-mes are one thing, implementing them is another. The task of a post-essentialist study of ethnicity would be easy if, as Keesing has argued, cultural essentialism were just the result of social scientists constructing some 'radical alterity – a culturally constructed other radically different from Us' (1994, 310). But the matter is not so simple, given that our own in-formants, too, use their own ideas about ethnicity to construct radical alter-ities about their own collective 'others' and for themselves. Turks in the Netherlands have ideas about 'Dutch society' and 'Dutch culture' just as much as native Dutch people have come to reify 'Muslims' and 'their culture'. If anthropologists are to break this spiral of mutual reifications, they must de-essentialize ethnicity empirically and will, in the process, test out how far this can be done.

In dealing with ethnicity in a post-migration context, we face a situation in which, to borrow Raymond Williams' (1976: 12) phrase, 'the problems of its meanings [... are] inextricably bound up with the problems it [is] being used to discuss.' To escape from this circularity, and to order the contributions, it has been most useful to de-essentialize ethnicity vis-à-vis three very old anthropological agenda: social cohesion, collective commitments, and the comparative project. To start with the first, we cannot assume that 'ethnic' minorities cohere *ipso facto*, as it were because they are 'ethnic'. This forms the bedrock of our enquiry, presented in Part One. Secondly, a de-essentialized approach to ethnicity must explore the ambiguities of commitments and identifications that people labelled as 'ethnic' minorities actually enter. Instead of some monolithic 'ethnic solidarity' we find, in Part Two, the cross-cutting cleavages that are so fundamental to social life in any plural society. That the cleavages of collective identities cut across each other in highly charged ways is exemplified most tangibly by pitching religious identifications against national ones. Finally, such an approach to ethnicity must grasp the old nettle of the comparative project. If our informants themselves trace 'cultural' differences to factors of 'ethnicity', we must ask how else such differences can be explained. This is the concern of Part Three.

Our collection as a whole thus aims at showing three things: how social cohesion is not some ethnically ordained or primordial 'given', but is constantly, and often discontinuously, re-made; how the value commitments among 'minority' communities are not 'ethnically' monolithic but struggle with, and make use of, the cross-cutting cleavages of plural social systems; and that cross-'ethnic' comparison, the oldest and least redeemed claim of anthropology, can be delivered on non-essentialist premises.

In the first Part, both Al-Rasheed and de Vries refuse to assume that 'ethnic' groups might continue to cohere in any unproblematic, quasi biological, sense. Instead, they ask how criteria of cohesion are re-interpreted, and social processes of cohesion actually change, in the post-migration arena. Madawi Al-Rasheed traces the ever-changing criteria of cohesion current among London's 'Assyrians'. Their collective constructions of an 'Assyrian ethnicity' have gone through extraordinary changes of emphasis, as well as historical self-understanding, during the post-migration period. Marlene de Vries shows how the social cohesion of the Turkish community in the Netherlands is recreated through new uses of, and views about, gossip among and about young women. What both authors press home is thus a processual view of 'ethnic' cohesion. This view attempts to trace the multifarious processes by which moments of cohesion are reconstructed, and it gives due weight to the discontinuities and normative discord that they entail.

The following Part, 'Commitments', takes on the most widespread empirical fallacy of the essentialized view of 'ethnic' culture. Given the cross-cutting nature of social identities, we must face the friction and tension, or analytically speaking the dialectic, of value commitments among 'ethnic' constituencies. Thijl Sunier, who writes of Turks in the Netherlands, extricates self-categorizations as 'Turkish' from self-categorizations as 'Muslim' and shows up a number of intervening variables, not least importantly those that go back to re-thinking at national government level. Lale Yalçın-Heckmann uses her ethnography of Turks in Germany to extricate processes of boundary maintenance on religious criteria from those based on national and 'ethnic' criteria. Her case study is especially innovative as it pitches the ambiguously 'German' or 'Christian' character of Christmas and New Year celebrations against an ambiguously 'Turkish' or 'Muslim' identification of the post-migration community. Gerd Baumann examines the interaction, in a multi-ethnic suburb of London, between Sikh, Hindu, Muslim and Christian religious ideas and shows how 'ethnic' categorizations based on religious criteria are re-negotiated by a dual strategy that articulates claims of converging with the other with claims of 'encompassing' (Dumont 1980) the other. What the three contributions combine to substantiate is, how collective commitments are re-negotiated in response to the cross-cutting nature of 'ethnic' and religious categorical boundaries.

The final Part, devoted to the comparative project, tests the empirical limits of de-essentializing 'ethnicity'. Cross-'ethnic' comparisons would be counterproductive, of course, if they were to re-inscribe essentialist definitions of 'ethnic culture'. Yet on the other hand, they do have to deal with populations that view 'ethnicity' as a reified force and indeed continue to labour, and even learn, under 'ethnic' constraints. Mies van Niekerk combines the history of Surinam's colonization with the history of its 'nation'-state independence to debunk 'ethnic' myths about differential social mobility. The differences between Creole and Hindustani Surinamese, she finds, have more to do with the myths of 'ethnic' identification than with the might of 'ethnic culture'. Flip Lindo is faced with a similar choice between 'ethnic myth or ethnic might' when he examines the 'ethnic' patterning of differences in young people's school attainment. While giving due weight to the different family dynamics prevailing in Turkish, as opposed to Portuguese, households in the Netherlands, he lays stress on the recent, that is post-migration, processes, rather than some essence of pre-migration cultural heritages. Indeed, the very fact of migration reconstitutes culture, as Al-Rasheed has reminded us at the beginning. That it does so even at the most personal level, is brought home by Marina Petronoti in the last of our comparisons: she has contrasted the relations between Greeks and Africans while they co-existed in Africa with their relations in post-migration Greece. This adds a reflexive twist to our deliberations on ethnicity: we cannot, as social scientists, ignore the reifications that the 'ethnic' version of the culture concept has spawned among the people we study. We have ways and means, however, to make these reifications the object of study, rather than its guide.

To draw conclusions from an edited collection can sometimes be a test of verbal ingenuity. In this case, however, it is easy. The contributors were agreed on one agenda: de-essentializing the anthropology of ethnicity cannot be done by writing programmatic articles. The argument must be made to stick ethnographically, and the ethnography has to take account of the fact that the very people we study are themselves beholden to reifications of ethnicity. These folk reifications pose serious analytical problems in a post-migration environment that shows all the cross-cutting cleavages of a plural society. Yet rationalization has not proceeded at the pace that Weber envisaged, and 'ethnicity', however the word is understood, has become a rationalization in its own right. One way out of this historical irony is an ethnographic approach that takes account of reifications of 'ethnicity' because they prevail, but at the same time treats them as data, rather than analytical guidelines. In doing so, we hope that an examination of ethnicity as constituted among informants will throw new light on social cohesion, collective commitments, and the comparative project, just as attention to the latter three may help to bring out the specificities of post-migration 'ethnic' action and thought.

For the planning and publication of this book, thanks are due to several institutions and individuals. In particular, we wish to acknowledge the support of the organizers of the conference, Drs. Cora Govers of the SISWO institute and Dr. Hans Vermeulen of the University of Amsterdam; Drs. Maryke Borghardt of SISWO who supervised the publication process; and Mrs. Ingrid van den Broek who helped us with her patient secretarial support.

References

Al-Azmeh, Aziz
    1993   *Islams and Modernities*. London: Verso.

Barth, Fredrik
    1994a Enduring and emerging issues in the analysis of ethnicity. In: Hans Vermeulen and Cora Govers (eds.), *The Anthropology of Ethnicity: Beyond "Ethnic Groups and Boundaries"*. Amsterdam: Het Spinhuis, pp. 11-32.

Barth, Fredrik
    1994b A Personal View of Present Tasks and Priorities in Cultural and Social Anthropology. In: Robert Borofsky (ed.), *Assessing Cultural Anthropology*. New York: McGraw-Hill, pp. 349-61.

Berger, Peter and Thomas Luckmann
    1967 *The Social Construction of Reality. A Treatise in the Sociology of Knowledge*. Harmondsworth: Penguin Books.

Comaroff, John and Jean Comaroff
    1992 *Ethnography and the Historical Imagination*. Boulder, Co.: Westview Press.

Keesing, Roger
    1994 Theories of Culture Revisited. In: Robert Borofsky (ed.), *Assessing Cultural Anthropology*. New York: McGraw-Hill, pp. 301-10.

Sahlins, Marshall
   1994   Goodbye to Tristes Tropes: Ethnography in the Context of Modern World
          History. In: Robert Borofsky (ed.), *Assessing Cultural Anthropology*. New
          York: McGraw-Hill, pp. 377-94.

Turner, Terence
   1993   Anthropology and Multiculturalism: What is Anthropology that Multicul-
          turalists Should Be Mindful of It? *Cultural Anthropology* 8(4): 411-29.

Vayda, Andrew
   1994   Actions, Variations and Change: The Emerging Anti-Essentialist View in
          Anthropology. In: Robert Borofsky (ed.), *Assessing Cultural Anthropology*.
          New York: McGraw-Hill, pp. 320-29.

Veer, Peter van der (ed.)
   i. p. *Nation and Migration: The Politics of Space in the South Asian Diaspora.*
          Philadelphia: University of Pennsylvania Press.

Weber, Max
   1978   *Economy and Society. An Outline of Interpretive Sociology.* (eds. Guenther
          Roth and Claus Wittich). Berkeley: University of California Press.

Williams, Raymond
   1976   *Keywords: A Vocabulary of Culture and Society.* London: Fontana.

Part I

Cohesion: not given but re-conceived

4 - trying to de-essentialize problem by
attacking assumptions of cohesion -
cannot assume that 'ethnic' minorities
cohere just ∴ they are ethnic

Presents a processual view of 'ethnic'
cohesion

In search of ethnic visibility
Iraqi Assyrian Christians in London

Madawi Al-Rasheed

Introduction

The study of ethnicity among immigrant groups in Britain has been largely guided by empirical evidence from the country's most visible ethnic minorities. Both the Afro-Caribbean and the South Asian populations provided important cases on which various theoretical formulations relating to ethnicity were tested (Anwar 1979; Benson 1981; Robinson 1986; Shaw 1988; Werbner 1990). Many of these conclusions, however, reflect the experience of highly visible groupings that have been subjected, since their early settlement in the 1950s and 1960s, to discrimination, stereotyping and stigmatization in various areas of interaction. While some studies have been dealing with the less visible 'minorities within minorities', such as Pakistani Christians in Britain (Jeffery 1976), African Asians (Robinson 1986), and Armenians (Talai 1989), this area remains far from fully explored. The Assyrian case is a contribution to this field.[1]

Assyrians represent a minority within a minority which saw no advantage in securing recognition as a distinct group, immediately after they had migrated to London, but that has since changed in ways which expand our perception of ethnicity. Until recently, Assyrians have maintained a low profile, so that the majority of the local population is unaware of their presence. When such an awareness is expressed, Assyrians tend to be confused with a wide range of other Middle Eastern immigrants such as Arabs, Iranians, Armenians and Kurds. The host society has learned to identify these groups as a result of continuous exposure by the media, following increasing political instability in that region and regular migration, especially, though not entirely, of some of the area's religious and ethnic minorities to safer countries in the West. The Assyrians of London, consequently, find themselves in a situation where they are mistaken for being Arabs or Muslims, two categories of immigrants which they try to distance themselves from. The construction of their ethnicity in recent years is highly influenced by their desire to distinguish themselves from Muslim Arabs, especially their Iraqi compatriots who belong to the Arab-Muslim mainstream population of the country.

Assyrians communicate their ethnic differences in specific contexts of interaction with the host society. Religion and language are used to draw the ethnic boundaries between themselves and the people from whom they constantly wish to be distinguished and with whom they are yet always confused. The majority of Assyrians are aware of the fact that they do not possess a hermetically distinguishable cultural tradition different from that of the Arab population with whom they coexisted for centuries. Those who adopt this view argue that they eat the same food as Arabs and subscribe to similar values and norms.[2] They give the example that they 'believe in family honour, protection and support of relatives, and respect of parents', all are values and norms shared with the Arabs of Iraq. Most Assyrians do not believe that they are the bearers of a totally distinctive culture, which is empirically rare except among groups living in complete isolation, a situation unlikely to be encountered in the modern world and in particular in the Middle East (Barth 1969). It is difficult to find objective differences in world view, values, norms, food and dress which could have set Assyrians as a cultural group apart from Iraqi Arabs whom I had the opportunity to know as a result of an earlier research project amongst them (Al-Rasheed 1992; 1993).[3] In the absence of a claim relating to the possession of a totally different tradition, Assyrians fall back on the most distinctive sub-elements of their culture: their Christianity and language. Both set them apart in their ethnic discourse from first, Iraqi Arabs, and second, other immigrants from the Middle East in Britain.

Religion and language constitute the fundamental cultural elements upon which Assyrians build a genre of ethnic narratives which is defined here as discourse used in social interaction between Assyrians and non-Assyrians, and built on a mixture of historical and mythical elements. The general theoretical approach adopted here derives from the assumption that ethnicity, as a system of classification, is a social process whereby both ethnic groups and identities are continuously constructed in specific contexts of interaction. Ethnic groups are, therefore, not fixed entities with distinct cultures awaiting description by outsiders (such as researchers), nor are they defined by clear-cut boundaries which are maintained and defended by the groups concerned. Rather, they are flexible categories whose definition can only be achieved through sustained observation of groups in action and interaction. This involves a situational analysis of ethnicity to manifest the essential variability in its significance for social relations in different social contexts and at different levels of social organization (Okamura 1981; Wallman 1983). However, my focus is not on the situations per se, but on the content of the interaction, the verbal communication, the messages which Assyrians incorporate in their ethnic narratives as they embark on a definition of themselves, reproduce their identity, and construct their ethnic difference. The unit of analysis is, therefore, the content of their ethnic narratives, embedded in their folk tradition.

Attention should be drawn here to an important distinction relating to people's perceptions of their ethnicity, that is their subjective classifications manifested in what they say and project about their ethnic belonging, and the analyst's interpretations and explanations of such native discourse. The two must not be confused. Assyrians' native discourse tends to be 'essentialist', inspired by beliefs in shared and inherent biological characteristics such as their reference to common blood, descent, primordial ties and physical traits. These projections are not unique to Assyrians but tend to be common also among other groups in the process of formulating their ethnic belonging. The inability of analysts to distance themselves from these emotive and powerful projections may lead to a reiteration and an unquestioning acceptance of native models, which become a substitute for a more detached understanding of ethnic phenomena. Already Weber has traced the constitution of ethnic groups to subjective shared beliefs in common descent on the basis of similarities of physical types or customs, or on the basis of shared memories of colonization or migration (Weber 1978: 389). Such an emphasis on putative primordial ties does indeed reflect native classifications and projections; these, however, cannot be taken at face value, but need themselves to be located in a wider sociological and historical context (Weber 1978; Comaroff and Comaroff 1992).

Another important methodological point relates to the fact that focusing solely on interaction diverts analytical attention from the wider social and historical contexts of ethnicity and thus implicitly disregards processes taking place beyond the grasp of the individual agent (Erikson 1991: 129). Erikson has rightly pointed out that we ought to investigate the historical and social circumstances in which a particular ethnic configuration has developed, and proceed to a precise localization in time, place and social scale of the ethnic phenomena (ibid.: 1993). One of the first propositions of Comaroff and Comaroff is to locate the genesis of ethnicity in historical forces that are simultaneously structural and cultural (1992: 50). It is this important aspect of analysis that deserves our attention first.

The wider context: History and migration

The understanding of Assyrian ethnicity requires a wider perspective in which this minority can be placed. Any analysis which starts from the moment Assyrians came to Britain (i.e. the post-migration situation) remains inadequate for it ignores the past experiences of migrants. These experiences not only influence their perceptions of situations in Britain, but also shape their relationships with their ex-compatriots who also migrated from Iraq and are now present in the host country. For this reason, I deal with two important aspects of the Assyrian experience, the history leading to migration, constructed from secondary historical sources, and the migration process itself, details of which are gathered from informants in London.

History
There are approximately 80,000 to 100,000 Assyrians living in present-day Iraq (Norris and Taylor 1992: 29). They are a Christian minority

whose members follow the Ancient Apostolic Assyrian Church of the
East, a church belonging to the Syriac-speaking group which has remained, in the Middle East, outside Roman Catholicism for centuries
(Atiya 1968; Arberry 1969; Coakley 1992). Most of the Assyrian population of Iraq consisted of the descendants of refugees who fled their
villages in Turkey during the First World War. The refugees were welcomed by the British mandate authorities in Iraq who began to recruit
them into what was known as the Iraqi levies, a military force designed
to protect the British air force bases in the country (Stafford 1935). As a
small Christian minority, Assyrians welcomed British protection in return
for loyalty and military service. Haunted by centuries of discrimination
within the boundaries of the Ottoman Empire, Assyrians reacted favour-
ably to their military recruitment into the levies . Some Assyrian nation-
alists looked to Britain to return them to their Turkish villages where
they could rebuild their lives under British protection. However, this did
not materialize, and most of the Assyrian refugees had to accept de facto
settlement in Iraq (Omissi 1989). Between 1918 and 1955, Britain,
through the levies, provided the main source of employment for Assyrians. The latter lived in military bases in relative isolation from the local
Arab population. During this period, the only contact between Assyrians
and Iraqi society was through suppressive military actions taken by the
former on behalf of the British.

   To understand why the London Assyrians want to distinguish themselves from Iraqi Arabs, one has to consider the antagonism between
this minority and the dominant Arab majority. The seeds of this antagonism lie in the Assyrian alliance with Britain during the mandate period
when they were used as a military force to suppress the dominant
population during its attempts to gain independence from the colonial
power. From the Assyrian point of view, the success of any Arab independence movement would jeopardize their position in Iraq. The majority preferred to live under the protection of Britain, a foreign power
seen to be committed at that time to the protection of minority rights.
Assyrians feared that the country's independence would not only ter-
minate their employment and threaten the source of their livelihood,
but would also result in their being punished and constantly reminded
of their collaboration with colonialism. From the Arab point of view,

Assyrians were never trusted and were always regarded with suspicion. Their existence on the periphery of Iraqi society, their association with the colonial power, and their demands for an autonomous Assyrian enclave in Iraq helped to enforce Arab suspicions and inflame hostility towards them.

This hostility found an outlet in 1933 when the Iraqi army, still in its infancy, decided to punish a group of Assyrian armed men who defected from the levies and were on their way to Syria to seek protection from France, the mandatory power there (Stafford 1935). The French authorities in Syria ordered the Assyrians to return to Iraq as requested by Britain. However, the Iraqi army, in a move uncoordinated with Britain, wanted to prevent the Assyrian armed men from re-entering Iraq. The Iraqi army opened fire, and it was estimated that 300 Assyrians were killed near a village named Simle (Atiya 1968: 286). Following the massacre, the Assyrian Patriarch was deprived of his Iraqi nationality and expelled to Cyprus with the approval of the British authorities (Omissi 1989; Joseph 1961). The massacre and the expulsion of the Head of the Assyrian Church had important consequences for Assyrian identity. During this situation of heightened conflict, Assyrians strongly emphasized their ethnic exclusiveness and increasingly began to see themselves as a group which could not coexist with the indigenous Arab population. After the massacre, Assyrian discourse centered on demanding international recognition of their ethnic and religious rights which they believed could only be achieved outside Iraq. However, their search for a home outside the country did not succeed. When Britain terminated its military presence in Iraq in 1955, which led to the Assyrian levies being disbanded, some Assyrian individuals and families opted for emigration after the failure of the plan to arrange their resettlement in another country on a mass scale.[4] Today, there remains a substantial Assyrian community in Iraq.

During the mandate period, Assyrian discourse on nationalism began to crystallize. After centuries of being defined as a *millet* (i.e. a recognized religious group) under Ottoman rule, Assyrians began to represent themselves to the international community as a 'nation'.[5] In addition to its distinctive religious and linguistic heritage, this entity was portrayed as possessing other national traits such as an 'invented' cultural tradition,

a myth of descent relating present-day Assyrians to distant ancient ancestors (the founders of the Assyrian Empire in antiquity), and a common historical experience with shared collective memories. These
definitions were inspired by their desire to create a new, secular, 'national' identity, while its main foundation had for centuries been dependent on their religion. This development was in line with the rising
hopes of minorities in the Middle East that followed the collapse of the
Ottoman Empire in 1918. Religious minorities aspired to the protection
of their rights under a new 'world order' in which it fell, effectively, to
the Western powers were to determine who counted as a minority, who
was to be protected, and where such protection was to be enforced.[6] It
is worth noting that Assyrians, like other religious minorities in the
Middle East, began to define themselves in secular terms in their search
for establishing themselves as a 'national' group.

This process was encouraged by proponents of western political doctrines and was further assisted by the British projections of the community, its history and identity, that followed World War I. These
projections were put forward by colonial officers, missionaries, and
other scholars who were interested in Assyrian history, language, and
tradition. A collection of English books (Wigram 1920, 1929; Srafford
1935) and reports were published at the time, all projecting an image of
a solid 'ethnic entity' with clear-cut boundaries that separated Assyrians
from others. A typical publication was that of Wigram (1920), which
portrayed Assyrians as a distinct group of Christians whose ancestors
were located in a distant past, that of the ancient Assyrians of Nineveh
and Babylon. The British 'essentialist' definition of the community was
popular among colonial army officers who propagated the myth that
Assyrians represented a continuation of the 'warrior race' of the ancient
Assyrian civilization, and this myth certainly seemed conducive to Assyrian recruitment in the British levies. The community itself responded by
incorporating such projections into their own ethnic discourse. This
interaction between British and Assyrian projections was highly effective, and it is still adopted with some modifications by Assyrians in the
post-migration context of Britain in the 1990s.

Migration

As a result of pioneer migration in the 1950s and 1960s, family reunions in the 1970s, and refugee migration in the past decade, there are approximately 4000 Assyrians living in the Borough of Ealing (west London). Early migration was motivated by a general sense of alienation from the mainstream population of Iraq, resulting from Assyrian association with the colonial power, a sense of fear of an unknown future under an Arab government wishing to establish itself as an independent state, and a desire to establish secure homes in a country where tolerance of ethnic and religious differences seemed well-established. These were historical circumstances which forced many individuals to search for settlement outside the country, not only in London but also in North America, mainly in Chicago and Detroit where substantial Assyrian communities exist today (Sengstock 1974), and in Europe especially in Sweden (Bjorklund 1981). However, while Assyrian links with Britain paved the road for an uneasy relationship with Iraqi society, this in turn facilitated their settlement in London.

At the micro-subjective level, immigrants gave a number of reasons to explain their migration. Many reported that they were motivated by a desire to find new economic opportunities in London after their main source of employment had dried up with the withdrawal of British forces from Iraq. Other migrants came to study and later opted for permanent settlement. Following a chain migration of related individuals, many Assyrians explained that the purpose of their migration was to join family members in London. However, in the last decade most immigrants arrived with the intention of seeking political asylum in Britain, especially at the time of the Iran-Iraq War in the 1980s and more recently the Gulf War in the 1990s. These late-comers are welcomed by already established immigrants, whose support is essential for the settlement of refugees.

Since the 1950s, Assyrians were successful in establishing a niche for themselves on the periphery of British society. Almost all immigrants lived in west London, where they founded their church, community centres and voluntary organizations that were meant to serve the immigrant population, and enforce group solidarity and cohesion through educational programmes and religious and social functions. The small size of the community meant that Assyrians were able to maintain face-to-face interaction with other members, and engage in primary networks which included only Assyrians. Excluding the work context, Assyrians did not, on the whole, attempt to build bridges with the host society. Their networks remained directed largely towards their own categorical group, and Britons, conversely, continued to be unaware of their presence.

During the period of early settlement, Assyrians invoked their ethnic ties to encourage the development of a strong communal spirit. It has to be noted that the first immigrants were predominantly from the British Royal Air Force Base at Habaniyya (Iraq). They had known each other well when they were in the British levies. Upon migration to London, this first group of immigrants developed a genre of ethnic discourse to explain to themselves, rather than to outsiders, why they must remain united as group. At that time, there were no identifiable communal goals or interests which this community wished to express apart from a plausible feeling of loss resulting from migration and a general anxiety over the potential dissolution of community ties. At first, then, Assyrians' projections of ethnicity were largely a response to their fears that the former co-resident community would be dissolved in an urban environment such as London. This was most important for the newly-arriving individuals who were searching for a community to turn to upon their arrival. Conversely, those immigrants settled already wished to re-build the solidarity and cohesion of the group in order to preserve kinship and communal ties.

At that time, Assyrian discourse concentrated on explaining why Assyrians as a migrant group should remain united. In co-operation with the church, community leaders tried to assemble a directory of the names and addresses of migrants so that they could be contacted for religious and social functions. The relatively secure economic conditions which the early immigrants encountered upon arrival in London, resulting from the demand for labour following the Second World War, meant that almost all members of the community found jobs, either prior to arrival, or immediately after settlement. Consequently, migrants did not feel the pressure to establish channels of communication with the host society which would introduce them as a recognized 'community', raise peoples' awareness of their presence, or press for its 'community' demands. Migrants used their own informal and family networks to find accommodation and employment, the most urgent issues for newcomers. Ethnic discourse was primarily directed towards internal consumption, and its purpose was to enforce a sense of belonging to a 'big family' of Assyrians who shared a common past, mainly through service in the levies, and were now in a foreign environment seeking economic success. So far, this had been achieved through co-operation and support from within the community, and this was also the way to pursue after migration.

It is obvious from the previous exposition that early immigrants began to organize themselves along ethnic lines the moment they arrived in London. An 'Assyrian Society of Great Britain' was founded in 1956. Its main objective was to ensure that all Assyrians present in London could be brought together for social and religious functions. The purpose was to strengthen collective solidarity and mutual support. Yet their conceptions of ethnicity were subjective, stemming from feelings of insecurity which can be expected in the wake of a migration process. Assyrians did not occupy a particular economic niche in London, nor were they organized to defend specifically communal economic or political interests. Assyrian ethnicity at that time was thus a subjective tool, and that was why the host society remained unaware of their presence.

In the 1980s and 1990s, all this began to change. Assyrians felt the need to adopt an extrovert version of ethnic identification to 'educate' the host society and raise its awareness of the presence of this invisible minority. Having secured ethnic solidarity among the community through the various associations created for the purpose, Assyrians now began to use these associations for the promotion of an Assyrian ethnicity mainly directed towards the host society. In the following section, I shall explain how the changing circumstances within the British host society have, over the last two decades, pushed Assyrians from an introvert and subjective ethnic identification to an extrovert display of Assyrian ethnicity.

Changing context in British society

From the 1960s on, the easy access of immigrants to Britain was reversed by a number of legal provisions which were meant to slow down, if not indeed halt, migration from the former colonies. Thus, the Commonwealth Immigrants Act (1962) regulated the flow of immigrants by imposing a voucher system and allowing family reunions for those already in Britain, but discouraged the migration of new-comers. Assyrian migration, too, was affected by the new legal circumstances, although they were not targeted as a group. With the exception of those who had close relatives already living in Britain, new immigrants could not be guaranteed settlement or residence rights. Some arrived on tourist or student visas and later applied for settlement. This was possible only if they found full-time jobs and if their employers were ready on their behalf to apply for work permits which alone could entitle them to residence rights. Another way of circumventing the obstacles imposed by immigration controls was for individuals to apply for asylum in Britain. This request had to be substantiated, and good reasons had to be found to convince immigration officers of the authenticity of any one case. It is in this specific context that Assyrian ethnicity came to be used as a tool to ensure that asylum cases were given due consideration. The community in London embarked on a campaign to enlighten the host society and raise public consciousness about their minority status in the country of origin. They emphasized the experience of persecution they had undergone, and their affinity towards Britain during their service in the Iraqi levies, intent upon reminding Britain of its historical responsibility towards this small group. Above all, Assyrian ethnic discourse centered on the claim that being a religious and linguistic minority in Iraq, their rights were not guaranteed, and in most cases they were discriminated against.

Another factor encouraging the search for increased ethnic visibility was the arrival of immigrants from Iraq and other Middle Eastern countries from whom Assyrians wished to distance themselves. In the late 1970s and early 1980s a series of political conflicts and ethnic violence fuelled emigration from the region: the Lebanese Civil War, the Iranian Islamic revolution, the Iran-Iraq War, and the Soviet invasion of

Afghanistan are but some examples of the instability in the area. More-over, ethnic violence against a number of minorities, such as Armenians and Baha'is in Iran, and Kurds in Turkey and Iraq, resulted in increasing numbers from these communities seeking refuge, not only in Britain, but also in other Western countries.

As far as the London Assyrians were concerned, this meant that they were beginning to be lumped together under a broad category of immi-grants, often referred to by the media, local authorities, and other agen-cies dealing with immigrants as 'Arabs' or 'Middle Easterners'. When different groups were competing over scarce local authority resources, this confusion did not help Assyrians to get a fair share, especially when these resources were in greater demand after the increasing arrival of Assyrian refugees. The community in London responded, in 1987, by organizing a campaign to explain to its local authority how 'different' Assyrians were from other Iraqis, and how they had to be treated as a separate community in their own right. This resulted in a positive re-sponse from the Ealing local authority which allocated a grant for setting up an 'Assyrian Cultural and Advice Centre', opened by the Deputy Mayor of Ealing. A photographic exhibition portraying different aspects of Assyrian history, culture, art and music accompanied the ceremony. The objectives of the Centre were summarized: 'to promote the welfare of the Assyrians with regard to matters of housing, education, health, immigration and counselling; to support Assyrian refugees; to promote the role of Assyrian women; to support Assyrian cultural, artistic and social activities; and to propagate Assyrian identity, culture, history and heritage and to establish good relations with local authorities and various ethnic minority groups and organizations' (*The Assyrian*, April 1988). This was their first successful attempt to make themselves more visible in London.

A new challenge to the community was the Gulf War of 1991. After the war, it was obvious that people in Britain began to distinguish between two categories of Iraqi immigrants, or more correctly refugees: Arabs and Kurds, the latter being the best-known group, given the publicity that their plight had attracted in the media. Being the third group and one of the oldest immigrant communities to have come from Iraq, Assyrians feared that they were not finding the attention they deserved, and that in most cases they were confused with either Arabs or Kurds. While it was generally taken for granted, in Britain, that Kurds represented genuine cases of refugees subjected to overt violence, Iraqi Arabs were considered a more suspect category because the causes of their flight were not as straightforward. This led to a series of arrests, detentions and deportations of Iraqi Arabs during the war. At the time, Assyrians felt caught between these two categories: the one regarded with sympathy, the other with suspicion. While they wanted to gain the sympathy awarded to the Kurds, they simultaneously wanted to dissociate themselves from the rather 'suspicious' group of Iraqi Arabs. Assyrians began, not only to search for ethnic visibility, but also to communicate their ethnic differences.

The previous exposition of the changing contexts in which Assyrians found themselves in the last two decades, was not meant to establish a causal relationship between the increasingly extrovert display of ethnicity and the various constraints imposed on Assyrians living in London. It was not the intention here to show that greater ethnic identification was directly caused by legal, economic, and political pressures or to conclude that Assyrian ethnicity was merely a response to the need to organize the group in order to defend their threatened communal interests. The situation is more complex. An analysis in terms of cause and effect can hardly account for the multiplicity of variables involved in the process of ethnic resurgence, or more accurately in the case of Assyrians' search for ethnic visibility, especially when their main purpose is to reject ethnic classifications predominant among the host society, that are due to ignorance, a desire for simplification, stigmatization, or a combination of such factors. When Assyrians assert their ethnicity in situations where they are labelled 'Iraqi Arabs' or 'Muslims', they react against a set of assumptions embodied in those labels. They then immediately embark on a narrative which sets the boundaries between themselves and those categories of immigrants more familiar to the host society.

The communication of ethnic differences

It is the interaction between Assyrians and non-Assyrians that provides the main context for the communication of ethnic difference. The exist-ence of the 'other' makes such communication important, if not essential as far as Assyrians are concerned. The 'others' torward whom Assyrians wish to draw an ethnic boundary are mainly Iraqi Muslim Arabs. The strong message underlying their ethnic discourse revolves upon assert-ing to the host society that they are neither Muslim nor Arab, but Chris-tians with a non-Arabic language. The following section illustrates how their narratives, placed in the context of interaction, re-establish these two points, and thus contribute to the construction of a separate Assyr-ian ethnic identity in London.

Religion

'We are not Muslims, we are Christians. Our church is the oldest church in the Middle East. We got it directly from Christ.'

'The main difference between us and them [Iraqi Arabs] is our religion. We are Christians. For centuries we have been prosecuted because of our religion.'

'To me, being an Assyrian is being a Christian.'

'When Christianity began to grow in the Middle East, we were the first to adopt it. We remained Christians in spite of various pressures. We are not Muslims.'

'We come from Iraq, but we are neither Arabs nor Kurds. We are Assyrians meaning that we are Christians.'

The statements above are extracts from field notes drawn from a section entitled 'Assyrian Ethnic Discourse' which included my observations and recordings of what Assyrians said when asked about their identity and ethnic belonging. To begin with, most Assyrians started by emphasizing their religious identity, a matter which the excerpts illustrate clearly. At a later stage in the conversation, they often embarked on an exposition, a constructed story or narrative of how they became Christians; how they preserved their religion amidst a predominantly Muslim popula-tion; and how this distinguishes them from other Iraqis living in London. They would emphasize, in the context of interaction with non-Assyrians, that they should not be confused with Arabs, the majority of whom are Muslims. If one made a comment that there were Christian Arabs in many Arab countries, for example in Syria and Lebanon, Assyrians would explain that these were not members of their own church but belonged to other Christian denominations such as the Catholic, Protestant, or Orthodox.[7]

Assyrians take pride in their own national church. They believe themselves to be the first nation to have accepted the gospel of Jesus Christ. This is propagated by their national leaders and intellectuals (Dadesho 1987: 12) and echoed in their conversation with non-Assyrians. Their justification for this narrative revolves around the claims that, first, they spoke the same language (Aramaic) as Jesus and his apostles spoke; and secondly, that the Assyrian community in Galilee was the first to make contact with Jesus. This religious mythology states that they came into contact with Christianity in the second year after the Ascension of Christ. His disciples Saint Thomas and Saint Peter are believed to be of Assyrian origin and are referred to as Mar Toma and Mar Shimoun Patros respectively. It is not the objective here to establish the historical truths behind such assertions, but to illustrate how religious knowledge about the past, be it historical, fictional, or mythical, is used in every day-encounters with non-Assyrians to construct an exclusive identity.

Assyrians insist that their Christianity did not arrive with missionaries from the West as it did in other parts of the world, but that it was their collective faith from the very beginning. They did not receive it from others, but were there to take it directly from Christ and his disciples. Such claims establish depth in time and imply historical authenticity, and they are woven together in short narratives that form an important dimension of Assyrians' ethnic discourse. The narratives form part of a folk tradition which is willingly told, expanded, shortened, modified and elaborated, depending on the time available to the interacting individuals and the purpose of social interaction. The following extract exemplifies one of the versions of these narratives. It is a story told by an Assyrian immigrant who regarded himself as a secular person, leaning ideologically towards Marxism, and who confessed that he does not believe in God. However, his ethnicity seems to revolve around the idea that he was born a Christian and that this is what makes him Assyrian:

'When people ask me where I come from, I say Iraq. If they say you are a Muslim, I say no, I am Assyrian, that is a Christian. I am also a Marxist, but Christianity is part of my identity, it is part of being Assyrian. All Assyrians are Christians, the two are inseparable. We are the first Christian community to have listened to Christ. Without it there will not be Assyrians. It is what makes me different from Arabs. Also, this is what makes me closer to Britain and its people. Before we had our own church in Ealing, Assyrians used to attend mass in Anglican churches. That was accepted. It would be unacceptable to go to a mosque.'

Religion does not only feature as a dominant pillar in Assyrian narratives, thus establishing a distinct ethnic identity, but is also an important organizational factor represented by the institution of the church. Historically, the Assyrian Church played an important role in propagating Assyrian identity and national aspirations, as it had been the institution dealing with Assyrian affairs under the Ottoman *millet* system. Today, the Patriarch remains the head of the community although his role is focusing increasingly upon the spiritual and symbolic, a process encouraged by the development of secular institutions and political parties. From his temporary See in Chicago, the Patriarch commands the deference of Assyrian communities including the one in London. Assyrians in Ealing indeed consider the Church not only as a religious institution, but also as the focus of their social life and ethnic identity. In the 1960s, the early immigrants did not have their own church building and many Assyrians attended mass in the local Anglican churches. They also used these churches for other religious ceremonies such as weddings, funerals and baptisms. An Assyrian woman, one of those who joined the local church, recalls: 'When I first arrived in Britain in 1970, I took part in my area's Anglican church. I used to go every Sunday for mass. I became a member of the Mothers' Union.'

However, this informant, like and many others, regarded this as a temporary measure until they would purchase their own church. Assyrians continued to feel the need to establish their own place of worship, listen to prayers in their own language, and have their marriages sanctioned by their own priests. Many Assyrians explained that without their own church building, they would be 'lost' in London, and that 'to pray, one can always go to mass in any church, but to be an Assyrian one must go to an Assyrian church'. They regarded the existence of a church as enhancing community solidarity and Assyrian ethnic belonging. For this purpose, an Assyrian Church Committee involved itself in fund-raising from 1985. This resulted in donations of £ 104,000 given by members of the community. A church building was bought in Ealing, close to where most Assyrians congregate (*The Assyrian*, April 1988). Since then, Assyrians felt that an important element in the preservation of their identity had been restored. Today, the church remains a symbol of Assyrian unity. It conveys on the community a religious identity defined in terms of belonging to one of the oldest churches in the world and enforces among Assyrians a sense of continuity with a distant religious past which has for centuries been the marker of Assyrian identity. Religion, to Assyrians, is thus not only a system of beliefs and rituals, but an important dimension in constructing who they are and what ethnicity they aspire to project.

Furthermore, Christianity provides some common ground between Assyrians and the British host society. Assyrians argue that they feel closer to Britain, its people and institutions in some areas of social life, and in particular in the domain of religious life, than they do to their compatriots from Iraq. A further relationship of affinity between Assyrians and Britain can be traced back, of course, to the time when Assyrians worked for the British mandate authorities in Iraq. Assyrian immigrants, especially those who came to Britain in the 1950s and 1960s, strongly believe in such affinities. Assyrians wish to be accepted in a way similar to how Italians, Poles and other white Christians have been integrated in Britain. This integration, however, remains a problematic issue which cannot be dealt with sufficiently in this paper. Suffice it here to say that, while religion is used in some contexts of interaction to draw a line of difference between Assyrians and Arabs, it is used in other contexts to blur the boundaries between Assyrians and members of the host society. Religion can be used for both inclusion and exclusion, depending on the social context that determines which aspect is invoked, be it overtly or in more subtle ways.

Language

While Christianity constitutes an important element in the construction of Assyrian ethnicity, it is also linked with Assyrians' linguistic heritage.

The liturgical language of the church remains until the present day Syriac-Aramaic, called *sopraya* in the Assyrian vernacular. It is worth noting that the church liturgy is incomprehensible to most lay Assyrians. It is spoken by a limited circle of religious personnel and only a small number of laymen who are associated with learning or theology. Yet the church liturgy is appropriated for the construction of a separate identity. Assyrians take pride in being the community 'which has kept this ancient language alive'. Such an assertion need not take account for the fact that most Assyrian immigrants are illiterate in this language. Mrs L., who regularly attends church service, explains why chanting prayers in Syriac-Aramaic, which she does not understand, is so special to her: 'Our prayers are in Aramaic. We chant it with our priest during communion. Although I do not understand it, it is so special to me. It is the language of Jesus Christ. It is what makes me Assyrian'.

The fact that this liturgical language is incomprehensible does not deter Assyrians from claiming that it is the language which distinguishes them from others. Syriac-Aramaic is a symbol used to establish authenticity rather than communication. It is also a sacred symbol as it is claimed to be the language of Christ. While this assertion is debated by scholars of religion and theology, most Assyrians seem to take it for granted.[8] In addition to its sacredness, Syriac-Aramaic is a symbol for the unity of the community. The church unites Assyrians all over the world through faith and rituals. Similarly, the language of this church becomes a symbolic field appropriated by Assyrians for the construction of a united community with shared religious and linguistic experiences.

While Syriac-Aramaic remains a sacred symbol enhancing Assyrian ethnicity and inscribing further the lines of distinction between them and Arabs or Muslims, their spoken language, commonly known as *suwaydiya*, is a shared medium of communication that continues to be used also in London. This spoken language affords a further claim to draw an ethnic distinction from Arabs. Assyrians argue that 'Arabs, speak Arabic. Arabic is their mother tongue. We are not Arabs. Our mother tongue is different'. Many indeed claim that there are continuities between their church language and their present-day vernacular and assert that they speak a corrupted form of Syriac-Aramaic. This is attributed, in the words of an informant, to '2000 years of intermingling with Arabs, Kurds,

Iranians and Turks', the dominant groups among whom Assyrians used
to live.

Although the majority of Assyrians in London are conversant in *suwaydiya* with varying degrees of proficiency, it has to be mentioned
that not all Assyrians are literate in this language. This is reflected in the
use of other languages, mainly Arabic and English, in some Assyrian
magazines and journals published in London. Furthermore, Assyrian
institutions, such as the church and the Assyrian Society of Great Britain,
usually send their circulars and leaflets in two languages: Assyrian and
English. Only middle-aged Assyrian immigrants are literate in their language as they were educated at the Assyrian School in Iraq during the
mandate period. Younger members of the community missed the opportunity of literacy in this language as the school curricula were
arabised after Iraq gained its independence. Consequently, it was
Arabic that became the language of literacy for all those who grew up
in independent Iraq. While many Assyrians did not have the opportunity
to gain literacy in their mother tongue, they seem to be determined to
ensure it for their children in London. It is not uncommon to find Assyrian parents who themselves cannot read or write the Assyrian language,
but insist that their children learn it. Most Assyrians speak to their children in Assyrian and object if the latter use English at home. Assyrian
motivation stems from the desire to maintain their distinctiveness as a
separate group from other Iraqi immigrants. In their ethnic discourse,
language features as an important element, not only in constructing
their ethnicity, but also in establishing a linguistic distance between
themselves and Arabs. An Assyrian immigrant put it explicitly when he
explained : 'We maintain our language here in London, we try to make
our children learn it, so that we are not considered Arabs or confused
with Arabs'.

For this purpose, there have been serious attempts to revive literacy
in the Assyrian language. This was achieved through setting up language
classes which used to be held at the Assyrian Club for four years in the
early 1980s. In 1986, a committee of learned members of the community
set up an 'Assyrian Language School', the purpose of which was to
promote not only knowledge of the language, but also of culture, history
and religion. At that time, the Ealing local authority agreed to offer

classroom space in one of the borough's local schools. This happened at a time when many London education authorities were responsive to the demands of ethnic minority groups to set up mother tongue classes. Assyrians used the school building for two years. They regarded the approval of the education authority as a victory for their ethnic distinctiveness and represented it as a serious recognition of their differences from the broad category of Middle Eastern immigrants who were concurrently establishing their infrastructures in West London. However, when the education authority demanded that they pay £ 150 to 200 for the four hours of teaching on Sundays, the Assyrian Education Committee decided to move the school to a local community centre where they were charged £25 per Sunday. Between 150 and 170 pupils are usually enroled for language tuition. The school also offers adult classes for both Assyrians and non-Assyrians. One of its five voluntary teachers expressed her views regarding her role in promoting and preserving Assyrian ethnicity in London: 'I want to help the community preserve its heritage. I see my role as more than just a language teacher. I want our children and adults to learn our songs, dances, tradition and history. When they speak our language, they stop being called Arabs'.

Conclusions

In this paper, I have argued that Assyrian ethnicity is a process which responds to changing contexts and experiences both in the home country and in the present situation in Britain. Assyrians remain conscious that in the past they were subjected to suspicion by the dominant Iraqi Arab society as a result of their association with Britain, the former colonial power. The ensuing ethnic and social distance to Muslim Arab Iraqis was perpetuated after their arrival in Britain. This history and the circumstances of their migration have greatly influenced the expression of Assyrian ethnicity. In the early 1960s, the community maintained a low profile and remained insulated in their ethnic enclave in Ealing. Their communal ties were strengthened for the purpose of preserving mutual support, solidarity, and contacts with other members of the community. The British public remained unaware of their presence as their ethnicity was largely a subjective experience based on insecurity and a fear of dispersal in an urban environment.

In the 1970s and 1980s, the context changed, firstly, as a result of legal measures to curb migration to Britain, later with the influx of immigrants from the Middle East, and more recently with the arrival of Iraqi refugees, both Arabs and Kurds. The host society and its institutions, such as local authorities and the agencies dealing with immigrants' services and needs, responded by developing their own categories and classifications of migrants. The categories 'Arab', 'Muslim', and 'Middle Easterner' acquired general currency. Later in the 1990s, 'Iraqi Arabs' and 'Kurds' surfaced in the media, as in other forms of discourse, to delineate two separate groups. Assyrians found themselves insufficiently recognized between these two categories. Consequently, they rejected the host society's classification and opted for a more 'positive' definition of themselves. Its main purpose was to correct 'misleading labels' and rectify what they regarded as 'false' classifications. Assyrians began their search for ethnic visibility in a country so far ignorant of their distinctiveness. This search led Assyrians to develop a genre of ethnic discourse that is punctuated by narratives situated in the interaction with the host society. The analysis of this discourse revealed that Assyrians rely on two factors to set up the boundaries between themselves and other categories of immigrants. Religion and language are constructed in such a way as to create distance between Assyrians and Arab immigrants from Iraq. In the absence of an easily identifiable cultural tradition that could separate Assyrians from Arabs, these two criteria assume the function, in Assyrian discourse, of justifying the claim to ethnic distinctiveness.

My concern here was not to establish the 'truth' about these narratives, but to investigate how past religious experiences and linguistic differences are used as symbols in the creation of a collective ethnic identity. However, it has to be mentioned that the approach adopted here does not entirely emanate from a constructivist standpoint that views people as capable of manipulating their identities, creating symbols, and constructing ethnic collectivities out of nothing. Assyrians, and for that matter many other ethnic groups, do 'create' or 'construct' an ethnic identity, but they must have a base to start from. A restrictively situational approach

like religious nationalism

that focuses solely on interaction must all too often ignore the wider historical contexts which influence the expression of ethnic distinctions. If circumstances request an assertion of ethnic belonging, then both the past and the knowledge relating to it can be activated, manipulated, and used to create distinct collectivities of people and groups. The circumstances in the Assyrian case manifested themselves in a series of historical changes, resulting from settlement in Iraq, migration to Britain, and the arrival of other immigrants from the Middle East with whom Assyrians were beginning to be confused. Assyrian ethnicity was thus to a great extent a reaction to the classifications and categories of the host society which paid little attention to internal religious and linguistic differences between various groups migrating from the Middle East. Given these complex interactions, I should emphasize the point that ethnicity cannot be considered the same 'thing' at different historical periods. Assyrians in Iraq adopted a definition of themselves which was mainly a response to changing historical circumstances which affected and defined their position in Iraqi society. In London, there were new circumstances that prevailed to encourage the development, first, of a subjective type of ethnic identification and later a more extrovert definition of the group. In all these situations, ethnicity remains rooted in space, time, and the prevalent circumstances of the person, the community, and the wider society in which it is displayed.

Notes

1. Contact with the Assyrian community started in 1991, and the research here used was conducted between March and September 1992. I am indebted to the various Assyrian voluntary organizations whose support made it possible to carry out field-work among the community in Ealing. I am also thankful to the Assyrian individuals who participated in the study. Finally, Nuffield College supported this research financially through research and travel grants. The study is based on detailed analysis of data collected from twenty Assyrian households, all resident in Ealing. Further, a number of community leaders, voluntary workers, teachers and Assyrian journalists and political activists were interviewed on issues relating to ethnicity, nationalism and group identity.

2. There is a small minority among the community in London who claim that Assyrians have clear cultural differences which set them apart as a cultural unit.

They fail, however, to give examples which are not related to religious differences. One of them, for instance, suggested: 'We are different from Arabs. We do not marry four wives'. This is, of course, related to the difference between Islam and Christianity rather than to a different 'ethnic' culture.

3.   Research among Iraqi Arabs was conducted in 1991. For further details, see Al-Rasheed 1992 and 1993.

4.   Between the two world wars, Assyrians kept sending representatives to the League of Nations with the objective of convincing the international community of finding a permanent settlement in a British colony or in French-mandated Syria. A committee was set up to investigate the possibility of settlement in British Guyana, Brazil, various African territories, Canada, and a number of other localities. After four years of investigation, the committee admitted failure to finalize a plan. It concluded that a settlement of Assyrians outside Iraq did not seem feasible and recommended that Assyrians retain their position as a minority in Iraq (Joseph 1961: 208).

5.   The position of Assyrians within the Ottoman Empire was similar to that of other Christians. The *millet* system gave the non-Muslim communities of the Muslim empire internal autonomy with respect to their property, inheritance, education, and family law.

6.   After the First World War, the victorious powers, mainly Britain and France acting under the umbrella of the League of Nations, raised the hopes of various minority groups in the Middle East (e.g. Armenians and Kurds). The latter wanted autonomy and a guarantee of their religious, cultural, and linguistic rights within the mandated territories. The majority of these demands, however, we never met.

7.   For a good discussion of Arab Christians, see Betts (1975).

8.   Coakley (1992: 369) argues that the Assyrian description of Syriac as 'Aramaic' is misleading if it is taken to mean that the 'Aramaic' New Testament contains Jesus' actual Aramaic words. The Syriac New Testament, he adds, is in fact a translation from the Greek, and exhibits a dialect different from that spoken by Jesus and his disciplines.

References

Al-Rasheed, M.
    1991   Invisible and Divided Communities: Arabs in Britain. In: *Arabs in Britain: Concerns and Prospects*. London: Riad El-Rayyes Books

Al-Rasheed, M.
    1992   Political Migration and Downward Socio-Economic Mobility: the Iraqi
            community in London. *New Community* 18, 4: 537-550.

Al-Rasheed, M.
    1993   The Meaning of Marriage and Status in Exile: The Experience of Iraqi
            Women. *Journal of Refugee Studies* 6, 2: 89-104.

Anwar, M.
    1979   *The Myth of Return : Pakistanis in Britain*. London: Heineman.

Arberry, A.
    1969   *Religion in the Middle East* (3 vols.). Cambridge: Cambridge University
            Press.

The Assyrian, April 1988, London.

Atiya, A.
    1968   *A History of Eastern Christianity*. London: Methuen.

Barth, F. (ed.)
    1969   *Ethnic Groups and Boundaries: The Social Organization of Culture Dif-
            ference*. Oslo: Scandinavian University Press.

Benson, S.
    1981   *Ambiguous Ethnicity: Interracial Families in London*. Cambridge: Cam-
            bridge University Press.

Betts, R.
    1975   *Christians in the Arab East*. Athens: Lycabettus Press.

Bjorklund, U.
    1981   *North to Another Country: The Formation of a Suryoye Community in
            Sweden*. Stockholm: Stockholm Studies in Social Anthropology.

Coakley, J.
    1992   *The Church of the East and the Church of England*. Oxford: Clarendon
            Press.

Cohen, A. (ed.)
    1974   *Urban Ethnicity*. London: Tavistock.

Comaroff, J and Comaroff, J.
    1992   *Ethnography and the Historical Imagination*. Boulder, Co.: Westview
            Press.

Dadesho, S.
    1987   *The Assyrian National Question at the United Nations*. Berkeley: California
            University Press.

Erikson, T.H.
    1991   The Cultural Contexts of Ethnic Differences. *Man* 26: 3-22.

Erikson, T.H.
  1993   *Ethnicity and Nationalism Anthropological Perspectives.* London: Pluto Press.

Jeffery, P.
  1976   *Migrants and Refugees: Muslim and Christian Pakistani Families in Bristol.* Cambridge: Cambridge University Press.

Joseph, J.
  1961   *The Nestorians and their Muslim Neighbors: a Study of Western Influence on their Relations.* Princeton: Princeton University Press.

Norris, H. & and Taylor, D.
  1992   The Christians. In: R. Tapper (ed.), *Some Minorities in the Middle East.* London: Centre of Near and Middle Eastern Studies, University of London.

Okamura, J.
  1981   Situational Ethnicity. *Ethnic and Racial studies* 4, 4: 452-63.

Omissi, D.
  1989   Britain, the Assyrians and the Iraqi Levies, 1919-49. *Journal of Imperial and Commonwealth History* 17, 3: 301-22.

Robinson, V.
  1986   *Transients, Settlers and Refugees: Asians in Britain.* Oxford: Clarendon Press.

Sengstock, M.
  1974   Iraqi Christians in Detroit: an Analysis of an Ethnic Occupation. In: B. Aswad (ed.), *Arabic Speaking Communities in American Cities.* Staten Island: Centre for Migration Studies.

Shaw, A.
  1988   *A Pakistani community in Britain.* Oxford: Basil Blackwell.

Stafford, R.
  1935   *The Tragedy of the Assyrians.* London: Allen & Unwin.

Talai, V.
  1989   *Armenians in London The management of social boundaries.* Manchester: Manchester University Press.

Wallman, S.
  1983   Identity Options. In: C. Fried (ed.), *Minorities: Community and Identity.* Berlin: Springer.

Weber, M.
  1978   *Economy and Society an Outline of Interpretive Sociology.* Berkeley: University of California Press.

Werbner, P.
   1990   *The Migration Process: Capital, Gifts and Offerings among British Pakistanis*. Oxford: Berg.
Wigram, W.
   1920   *Our Smallest Ally: A Brief Account of the Assyrian Nation in the Great War*. London: Bell and Son.
Wigram, W.
   1929   *The Assyrians and Their Neighbours*. London: Bell Press.

The changing role of gossip: towards a new identity?

Turkish girls in the Netherlands

Marlene de Vries

Introduction

Turkish girls and young women in the Netherlands[1] speak of social control,[2] in particular gossip, as one of the main factors contributing to their ethnic identity – in this case, their sense of being Turkish.[3] These girls live in the midst of compatriots who feel entitled to keep a beady eye on their behaviour. Consequently, the girls are often the subject of gossip of a fairly pernicious nature, which may have drastic repercussions. This type of gossip and the consequences it can have are considered as 'typically Turkish' by many Turks in the Netherlands. The gossip generally centers on such topics as the girls' chastity and the degree of their so-called 'Dutchification' (*vernederlandsen*). On the one hand, such gossip proves highly irritating to girls who value their personal freedom and do not wish to have all their actions constantly monitored. On the other hand, they wish to retain their sense of being Turkish. In this chapter, I shall first give a brief survey of the general context of Turks in the Netherlands. Next, I shall deal with the following questions: how does gossip function among Turks in the Netherlands, and what circumstances lead to gossip in this group becoming such an effective weapon to enforce social conformity? Why is the gossipee, or person gossiped about, so vulnerable in this situation? Is this limited to Turkish girls in a post-migration setting, or is the phenomenon more widespread? To what extent is the phenomenon a product of its time? I shall then argue that we can detect the first faint whispers of change in this mechanism: whereas gossip has been a factor contributing to group integration it appears to be turning, under the influence of multi-faceted social changes, into a factor leading to group disintegration. In conclusion, the much-coveted freedom seems to have become a more realizable dream – at least for some Turkish girls. This, however, requires a redefinition of their own identity.

I shall address these questions with reference to my research carried out among Turkish girls and young women and I shall, in the process, relate them to some theoretical notions taken from the social science literature dealing with gossip. It should be said, however, that this literature is rather thin on the ground, and there are remarkably few explicit studies of this phenomenon. I shall discuss in particular the ideas of the American anthropologist Merry (1984) and the British anthropologist Gluckman (1963, 1968).

Turks in the Netherlands: general context

The first Turkish immigrants in the Netherlands arrived around 1960. In 1964, the Dutch authorities established a so-called 'recruitment agreement' with Turkey. Thereafter, the number of Turkish workers in the Netherlands increased rapidly. Between the late 1960s and the early 1970s there was a peak in the Turkish labour migration. In 1974, when there were more than 50,000 Turks in the Netherlands, a recruitment stop was proclaimed. As a result, it became impossible to enter the Netherlands (legally, at least) as a labour migrant. But in the meantime, many Turkish men had started to let their wives and children come over from Turkey to the Netherlands. These family reunions continued, and reached their height in 1980. By then, the Turkish population had grown to 120,000 persons. Over the first half of the 1980s, the Turkish immigration rates declined as less and less families still had to be reunified. From 1985, however, the rates started to rise again as the children of labour migrants started to contract marriages: many of them chose a partner from Turkey. Over the last few years, the immigration rate has fallen again.

In 1994, there were about a quarter of a million Turks living in the Netherlands. This figure includes their offspring born in the Netherlands, but two out of three Turks residing in the Netherlands still have birth-places in Turkey (Böcker 1994: 2-3). While the vast majority of Turkish youngsters under the age of 18 years has been born in the Netherlands, most of the youngsters older than 18 years have been born in Turkey (Böcker ibid.: 6).

Most of the labour migrants come from families of petty peasants. Some of them had moved to a Turkish town before their migration to western Europe. Most of them have had little schooling: some three quarters only finished elementary school. A small minority finished secondary school or a higher education in Turkey. The vast majority, after arrival in the Netherlands, performed unskilled or semi-skilled jobs, mainly in the industrial sector. Due to economic developments, many of them became unemployed in the late 1970s or early 1980s, and have remained so until now. Youngsters who came to the Netherlands for family reunions in the 1970s or 1980s reached a higher level of education, either in Turkey or in the Netherlands, than their parents had done. But their average level is still not very high, and considerably lower than that of the Dutch population. Youngsters who have been born in the Netherlands, however, seem to reach a far higher level than their older brothers and sisters, who spent part of their life in Turkey (Böcker ibid.: 21). Many of them are still in full-time education. The sample on which this chapter is based reflects the general background given above. It consists of 25 girls and young women, aged between 16 and 25.

How does gossip become an effective means of social control?

Gossip may be universal (see Gluckman 1963: 312; Stirling 1956: 262), but it takes many forms. It varies in nature from the mildly ironic to the downright malicious. Its functions vary likewise. It may be simply chit-chat that is soon forgotten, in which case the results are limited to short-lived entertainment enjoyed by the gossipers. But it can also prepare the way for further action, such as ignoring or boycotting the gossipee, or even threaten their standing as a member of a national community. In such a situation, gossip functions as a crucial link in the long chain of measures operating as social control. This chapter deals with the latter type of gossip. It is of a fairly malicious nature and entails a strong measure of control and threat. This is the sort of gossip that Turkish girls and young women in the Netherlands are frequently the subject of, and that often exerts a decisive influence on both their social and their private lives.

Most girls live surrounded, to varying degrees, by compatriots who see it as their task to keep watch over the girls' behaviour: they must be chaste and remain Turkish, that is, not become 'Dutchified' (*vernederlandst*). The relevant standards are set by fairly conservative people. If a girl does not behave impeccably according to conservative standards, she can be assured that she will become the subject of gossip. This will be directed, not only against her, but also against her parents. For they, according to the gossipers, have failed to keep their daughter under control. It is this result, the blemishing of the parents' reputation, that girls fear most, for it loads them with an enormous sense of guilt. Their loyalty towards their parents is often intense, and this alone can suffice to deter them from conduct sanctioned by gossip. From a Dutch point of view, this is usually fairly innocent behaviour, such as joining classmates to go downtown after school, talking with a male classmate or colleague in the street, or having a close friendship with a Dutch girl. In fact, many Turkish girls cannot see anything wrong with such behaviour *per se*, and they refrain from it, not so much because of a deep conviction that it is wrong, as out of fear of unpleasant repercussions. Importantly, once the family reputation has been tarnished by gossip, this may lead to further sanctions. These may include being looked down upon by compatriots, sanctions in the private sphere such as beating, house arrest, an (early) arranged marriage, or an interdiction on attending school. It therefore seems fair to state that gossip, and other forms of social control associated with it, form a serious obstacle to the individual emancipation and autonomy of many Turkish girls. As they themselves put it, they have a sense that someone is always 'looking over their shoulders', that they 'live in an open prison', and that their lives are being 'controlled by others' (de Vries 1987).

Gossip, of course, does not always have to function as such an effective instrument of social control. Further, even within the group investigated, there were slight variations in the effect of gossip and the vulnerability of the gossipees. What, then, are the circumstances that make for effective gossip?

The work of Merry (1984) offers some valuable starting-points here. Merry specifically describes these circumstances by means of four hypotheses. It is not possible here to test these hypotheses: a far larger and more varied sample would be required in order to do so. I propose, however, to illustrate them with my research material and to provide some comment upon them. The hypotheses are as follows:

1. The impact of gossip and scandal is greater in more bounded social systems in which the costs of desertion or expulsion are higher and the availability of alternative social relationships less.
2. The impact of gossip and scandal is greater in social settings where the members of the local system are more interdependent for economic aid, jobs, political protection and other social support.
3. The impact of gossip and scandal is greater when it has the potential of producing a community consensus that can be converted into a variety of collective actions such as public shaming, ridicule, expulsion or death.
4. The impact of gossip and scandal is greater when normative consensus about the behaviour in question is more extensive (Merry 1984: 296).

How far, then, can these hypotheses be substantiated from the point of view of older Turks and of the younger generation of Turkish girls, be they observed as gossipers or gossipees?[4] The first two hypotheses postulate that the influence of gossip is primarily felt in a close community in which people are highly dependent upon each other for various social needs. Clearly, not all Turks live in equally close communities. The most tightly-knit networks are those where many relatives and people from the same village or region in Turkey are living in the same neighbourhood (Böcker 1994: 12). The more Turkish girls are exclusively dependent upon their contacts within such an immediate circle of relatives and the surrounding network of Turkish acquaintances, the greater the effect of gossip and its concomitant results (de Vries 1987: 87-88). This dependence, albeit manifest in varying degrees, is quite a common feature, to which contacts with Dutch people are no alternative. Many Turkish parents indeed discourage their daughters, in a more or less forthright manner, from developing close ties with Dutch people. Many dread that their daughters may become infected with Dutch, that is, unsuitable ideas (de Vries 1987: e.g. 24-5, 50 and 111). Many girls more or less internalize this attitude of their parents, which explains why, despite their contacts with Dutch contemporaries, many continue to feel insecure, restricted and 'not themselves' when in the company of Dutch people (de Vries 1987: e.g. 24 and 98-103).

This parental policy of discouragement has been described as a 'psychological commandment against integration' by Graafsma and Tieken (1987). They describe how, for the first cohort of immigrants, the actual move and the subsequent period give rise to feelings of insecurity, anxiety and regret. Ambivalence, and not infrequently also fear and suspicion, are thought characteristic of migrants' attitudes toward the new country. In due time, they are thought to develop their own peculiar migrant culture, which can be interpreted as a kind of defence mechanism; it is the attempt to remain internally stable and not to disintegrate socially. People, in this model, try to recreate the old, safe environment; consider whether or not to return to their former country; and at the same time grow attached to a 'permanent temporary stay' (Graafsma and Tieken 1987: 31). Newcomers indeed have no great regard for Dutch norms and values, especially those concerned with personal relations. Furthermore, experiences involving discrimination or insulting remarks from Dutch people may well add to the migrants' continuing sense of remaining outsiders (Risvanoğlu-Bilgin et al. 1986: 87 and 99-101). Serious conflicts of loyalty may result from all this: to become involved in the new country can come to seem like disloyalty to the old one. This is not only a question of individual personality but is also affected by fellow migrants who may demand loyalty to certain ideals. While these mechanisms restrict personal freedom, they do in exchange offer a certain subjective security. Many Turkish girls encounter this strategy of discouragement from their parents, and increasingly so as they grow older and are time and again reminded of the fact that they are different from their Dutch contemporaries. Thus, to meet their needs for social imbedding they become increasingly dependent on compatriots who form part of their parents' network or who are at least acceptable because of their way of life and ideas (de Vries 1987:

45-46). Where there are no substitutes for these relationships and the dependence that they create, a person is rendered more than usually susceptible to gossip and loss of reputation.

Merry's second hypothesis discusses interdependence, not only for social support, but also for financial help, jobs, and political protection. In the case of the girls I studied, however, this was primarily a question of social support and, above all, a sense of belonging. Dependence on compatriots in the political or economic field occurs relatively rarely (apart from specific financial dependence of daughters on their fathers or unemployed married women on their husbands), and gossip therefore does not have such a great influence in these areas. In all probability the situation is different for men. To substantiate Merry's third hypothesis let me cite briefly the following case. It exemplifies the extent to which someone, in this case a man, can be affected by gossip because of economic dependence on compatriots, and it further shows him especially vulnerable by dint of his daughter's behaviour. Mr H. ran a small business selling Turkish goods in Amsterdam and was mainly dependent on Turkish clients. He had a sufficient number of them, because the shop was in a largely Turkish neighbourhood. According to my informant, it comprised mostly country people from one region in Turkey and was rather conservative. The shopkeeper had two teen-age daughters: lively, 'modern' girls, both of them attending secondary school and following courses of a fairly academic orientation. From time to time they would help their father in his shop. The Turkish neighbours did not approve of the girls' behaviour, which they said was far too free, and they pronounced the father responsible for this. However, he was not prepared to order his daughters to alter their behaviour. A gossip campaign in the neighbourhood resulted in the shop losing most of its Turkish clientele, and Mr H. was forced to sell his business.

In general, Merry's third hypothesis refers to severe sanctions that may be imposed once a person has already become the subject of gossip and scandal. Gossip is indeed all the more effective if it results in negative sanctions, that is, if it functions as a kind of connecting link on the long route of social control (Bergmann 1987: 195). Yet gossip may result not only in community sanctions, but also in private ones. For example, there may be penalties imposed by the parents or the husband, such as beating, house arrest, restriction on school attendance, being sent back to Turkey, having an arranged marriage – or being threatened with any of these (Brouwer et al. 1992; Önen 1989: 12). Here, too, the rule applies: many girls will not want things to go so far, but will instead anticipate sanctions by refraining from contentious behaviour 'at least in public' and by taking care not to become the subject of gossip in the first place. With this in mind, we can now add to Merry's third hypothesis which will then read as follows:

The impact of gossip and scandal is greater when it has (or people think it has) the potential of producing a community consensus that can be converted into a variety of collective actions such as public shaming, ridicule, expulsion or death, or in private sanctions such as beating, house arrest, forbidding school attendance, sending back to country of origin, marrying off, or threatening with such a sanction.

It seems appropriate here to clarify the use of the term 'community' which has now occurred several times. What is the size of the community that reaches a certain consensus and that has the power to apply sanctions? Are we dealing with Turks in one particular district or city, or with 'communities' in a wider sense? Böcker (1986: 63) points out that what is generally taken to be 'the' Turkish community is in fact a 'collection of loosely-connected networks'. It requires further research to investigate the precise consequences of such a structure in the functioning and spread of gossip. To what extent and under what circumstances do members of different networks participate in a single gossip campaign? Limited by numbers as my data are, they do contain certain indications that the gossip stories and the consensus they express command a fairly wide public, and at any rate extend further than the circle of relatives and close acquaintances of the gossipee. Merry's fourth hypothesis is connected with this factor of reach: the impact of gossip and scandal is thought greater when normative consensus about the behaviour in question is shared by more people. While my data do not allow for a decisive assessment, they lead me to suspect that this hypothesis is not generally valid. It may not be the number or range of people denouncing a certain type of behaviour that is decisive, but the relationship of the gossipee to these people. The closer the bonds and the more dependent the gossipee is on the gossipers, the more keenly will he or she experience the gossip and scandal. In fact there appears, at least in the case of my research population, to be an intervening variable in this connection. That is the attitude of the parents, or the husband, of the gossipee. A Turkish girl is primarily vulnerable to gossip if it threatens social discredit to her parents and possibly her wider family, and, notably, if this worries her (de Vries 1987: 90). If the latter condition does not apply, then the vulnerability of the girl is far less, even though her behaviour may be condemned by many compatriots. To clarify the link, one may consider three variations. (1) The girl's family and the gossiping compatriots agree that the behaviour in question is unacceptable. In such a case the impact of gossip will be greatest. (2) The girl's family and the gossiping compatriots do not agree about the unacceptability of the behaviour in question. The family considers it acceptable and pays no attention to the gossip. In this case the impact of the gossip and scandal upon the girl will be limited. (3) The girl's family and the gossiping compatriots do not agree about the unacceptability of the behaviour in question. The family thinks it is acceptable but does not want this known outside the family circle, to avoid becoming the subject of gossip. In this case, the impact of gossip upon the girl will be greater than that under (2), but less than under (1).

The points on which my findings support Merry's hypotheses can be summed up as follows. A Turkish girl will be more affected by gossip and scandal, the more she lacks alternatives, especially in the social sphere. In the community from which she comes there must be a certain consensus regarding norms and values. Those who gossip also need other effective means of social control, and they must be able to apply (or allow) further sanctions. It is, to quote Merry, '...those in the middle of the social spectrum ... who are most concerned about gossip and most vulnerable to its consequences.' The least vulnerable are the rich and powerful or those with an otherwise elevated status; and also those on the periphery of local society or those with supportive contacts outside the local social system (Merry 1984: 272 and 295-6). In my research sample this limited vulnerability is illustrated by several girls whose parents maintained little contact with compatriots in their vicinity and in that sense did not occupy a middle position in the social spectrum. An example may serve to illustrate such a case. It concerns two schoolgirls,

Güllü and Gonça, who are 16 and 17 years old respectively. Güllü was two years when she came to the Netherlands, whereas Gonça was born here. Both girls have 'sinned'. It is the same transgression, but the impact differs for the two girls because of the different positions they occupy within the local Turkish community. They both secretly had a (Turkish) boyfriend and both had been caught red-handed by a compatriot, when they were talking (and probably kissing) the boy in the street. For Güllü the consequences were quite considerable. In the place where she lived everyone gossiped about her, and she noticed many side effects; for example, the daughter of friends of her parents was no longer allowed to come to her house. She became anxious about whether or not, in view of her reputation, she would ever be able to make a suitable marriage with a Turk. Güllü's parents retained many contacts with compatriots, and this rendered her highly vulnerable. In contrast, the parents of Gonça did not. As she reports: 'My parents never had a lot of contact with Turks here, they are so different. They are only friends with the parents of my girlfriend A., but they come more from our part, you see, the west [of Turkey]'. I never heard anything about gossiping among other Turks after she had been seen with her boyfriend, nor about any other detrimental effects (de Vries 1987: 87).

Such observations put an important qualification on the circumstances under which gossip can be an effective means of social control. Clearly, this consideration is not limited to Turks in the Netherlands, or indeed to migrant groups. Admittedly, there are some migrant groups that appear to fit Merry's conditions preeminently. In particular, these are groups with a tendency to emphasize the differences between themselves and the indigenous population, because they consider their own way of life, norms and values, to be superior and wish to preserve them – sometimes even against their better contextual judgment. In a formal social context, there is usually little that people can do against the threatening influence of an unacceptable lifestyle or morality; informally, however, they can reject these by various types of social control, of which gossip is one. This may hold all the more when the migrant group in question has not been in the new country for long, or as long as the cohort who migrated as adults retains influence over the migrant group as a whole. It is under such conditions that gossip can become a

formidable weapon to enforce social control. To illustrate the point, one
may think of Italians in the United States during the 1920s (Ware 1977),
Hindus from Surinam in the Netherlands (Mungra 1990), and Moluccans
in the Netherlands (van Wijk 1985; Bartels 1989).[5]

The phenomenon as a product of its time

What we have seen above is that gossip provides a means to appeal to
communal values; people gossip about the fact that the gossipee has not
conformed to the accepted behaviour of the community in question.[6]
Thus gossip, provided it meets certain conditions, contributes to unifor-
mity of behaviour and thereby to a certain group cohesion. This said,
however, gossip should not be seen as a cause of conformity and ethnic
solidarity; rather, the values held and the gossip taken to heart condition
each other. It was Gluckman (1963, 1968) who pointed out that gossip
can have an integrating function for a group. This, however, is a latent
function – most gossipers do not gossip with the manifest intent of holding the group together. Their immediate motivation will often be considerably less noble: jealousy, revenge, projection of their own dissatisfaction, the need to feel better than others, and so forth. My material
confirms Gluckman's proposition, but at the same time it contains sug-
gestions to the opposite: gossip and its impact may, in the long run, have
a disintegrating effect on the group.[7] This, at least, is my somewhat
tentative interpretation of the reactions of Turkish girls. If we listen
carefully to what these girls say, we hear two things. On the one hand,
angry stutterings and expressions of rage or powerlessness; on the other
hand, the desire to remain Turkish and to form part of a group whom
they may sometimes curse but with whom they also feel closely connected. Naturally, they sometimes condemn the old-fashioned and un-
sophisticated morality of their gossiping compatriots, with whom some
of the girls can no longer easily identify. Yet in its place they propose
not a 'Dutch', but a 'modern Turkish' morality. None of the girls wished
to become 'Dutchified', although no-one in fact managed to explain the
precise difference between a 'Dutch' and a 'modern Turkish' way of
behaving. At all events, they project a strong need for continuity. But

their need for change, in the sense of having fewer restrictions put on
their behaviour, is also great. Confusion, conflicting feelings, and clashes
of loyalty are the result.

Such feelings of ambivalence are not, of course, unique to these girls.
They are typical of a new situation: on the one hand, the recent social
developments give rise to new ideas, in the case of Turkish girls primarily ideas about freedom of action; on the other hand, loyalties, affections
and codes of conscience are still imbued with long-standing attitudes.[8]
The Turkish girls whom I interviewed were steeped in both discontent
and conformity. Nonetheless, this conformity seemed largely a matter of
appearance – a matter of behaviour rather than of attitude. It would be
inappropriate, thus, to speak of a profound internalization of the prescribed
rules of behaviour. Many of these behavioral codes arise from the ideal of
virginity. This ideal itself is not up for discussion, yet the rules that are
deduced from it are. Not many Turkish girls appear to contest the notion
that virginity should be preserved until the wedding night.[9] But that this
should imply that you may never indulge in out-of-school activities,
must always be on your guard, and cannot decide upon anything in your
own life – that is going too far.[10] In such an attitude one may detect the
faint whispers of change.

Given his characteristically functionalist preoccupation with group
cohesion, Gluckman failed to discern this possibility: yet if conformity
is no longer based on internalized convictions and does arouse increasing resistance, then this conformity itself is doomed to disappear. In such
a situation, one should not exaggerate the effectiveness of gossip as a
means of social control. Gossip can be a strengthening factor of group
and ethnic solidarity only if the values it expresses command a genuine
moral commitment within the community.

Given these observations, I should like to consider the following hypothesis, provided as an extension to Gluckman's argument: Gossip
and its impact may be one of the factors contributing to a process of
group disintegration.

The notion that gossip does not always promote group cohesion or
function as an effective means of social control, is not new: it emerges
in several studies.[11] The factors that are usually mentioned in this

connection are the absence of strong networks or of a moral consensus, and also the inability, or lack of motivation, to act as a group and allow gossip to evolve into group action. What these studies leave unclear, however, is whether or not gossip in the groups described originally fulfilled a group-stabilizing function, and, if so, how its function changed to render it a factor in the process of group disintegration. This is the question I am here concerned with, and suspect that in the case of certain migrant groups, this is a question of phases. To start with, gossip sustains group cohesion, but at a later stage it in fact works as a de-stabilizer. To test this hypothesis, one would require research that studies gossip over a long period, preferably over several generations. I know of no such study. The only one approaching it is that of Bartels (1989) who studied several generations of Moluccans in the Nether-lands, and it would seem from this work that my hypothesis could be confirmed. I shall return to it below.

A more detailed study, however, would be necessary to answer my question fully: whether, and if so how, social control mechanisms can work in a dynamic way and come to function as agents of social change (van Doorn and Lammers 1969: 276). One could question this line of enquiry by objecting that discontent as such need not threaten group cohesion. Social control may always arouse opposition, quite simply because it restricts people's freedom of action. This may be annoying for individuals, but it need not have negative consequences at the group level. It indeed does not need to; but it may. The feelings of discontent observed among the Turkish girls are, of course, not in themselves sufficient to remove them from community censure or even ensure them greater autonomy. The key question, however, is to what extent such feelings of discontent may destroy the 'force of the self-evident'. How far will the girls in question shake off the restrictions they find too limiting, and in particular, to what extent will they call into question the legitimacy of so far-reaching an influence from others upon their own lives? Such developments would severely restrict the authority of gossipers, and hitherto collective norms and values would tumble like a pack of cards. Gossip would acquire a kind of boomerang effect. So far, it has not come to this, at least not on a scale worth mentioning. Yet we do have a few small indications of a development in the direction here sketched.

The future: the changing role of gossip

Various writers express the wish felt by many Turkish girls (and in fact by boys, too) to leave the neighbourhoods where many compatriots live nearby. One reason given for this is that they wish to avoid the social control of the group.[12] And while it cannot yet be ascertained to what extent this wish will result in deeds, it can certainly be seen as a practical intention to achieve greater autonomy. This also applies to girls who run away from home; most of them give as their reason the constricting rules and the desire for greater autonomy. But although the number of girls who run away is increasing, they still form a small minority, and we do not speak here of the 'average' Turkish girl (Brouwer et al. 1992: 13 ff.). Important as this type of consideration may be, a more decisive factor should lie in the wider social influences that Turkish girls experience. In all probability, these will lead to at least some of the girls reacting with greater autonomy and independence in the face of gossip and its consequences. It may be useful, in this regard, to consider a group where similar processes have taken place. Bartels (1989) has demonstrated how gossip and its consequences gradually lose their impact among what he terms the 'third generation' of Moluccans in the Netherlands. This is the first cohort to be born in Holland and whose youth was spent, to a certain extent, in camps.[13] The development was part of a more comprehensive process in which ideas concerning autonomy and privacy gained increasing prevalence. Rigid social control became less and less acceptable to members of this cohort, and for some of them this provided the direct reason for their leaving the group and settling outside the Moluccan district. The changing geographical position among Moluccans makes it ever more difficult to exert social control. Furthermore, the young people, have often – almost without knowing it – picked up other ideas. There is a growing emphasis on privacy and on making one's own decisions. Visits are no longer made unannounced but only after arrangement. Such things, in the eyes of the parents, are unacceptable and selfish. Attempts to exert social control in this situation are not only less effective, they are also less direct. Of course, jealousy and gossip are still present – in particular in the local communities – but it is less often that they result in communal action or open threats, the use of force or accusations of witchcraft (Bartels 1989: 301-322). The restriction on behavioral alternatives, which is necessary for shaping and preserving a community, does indeed appear to be '...a social and thus in consequence an unstable and vulnerable acquisition' (Cachet 1990: 36).

A similar change in the function of gossip, namely from contributing to group integration to furthering the process of group disintegration, can be seen among the group of Turkish girls whom I studied. The change is not as clear as that among the third cohort of Moluccans. Yet despite the differences between the two groups it would seem as if a similar development were almost unavoidable. As in the case of the young Moluccans, one can sense and feel the impact of an increasing individualization. It is quite probable, also, that young Turks in the Netherlands will show increasing diversification by their levels of education and socio-economic position. As social diversity breeds normative diversity, so consensus about norms and values will gradually lessen. Barriers that prevent intercourse with people outside the circle of family and friends may gradually break down under the influence of increasing social diversification. Geographical spread, too, appears set to increase. In such a situation people will be able, more easily than before, to withdraw from the Turkish enclosure if gossip becomes too irritating. Changing one's network becomes an alternative to conformity (Hannerz 1967: 58). Such factors, together with expanding opportunities in various fields, can create a climate in which gossip may certainly flourish, but the gossiper no longer has the means to exert effective social control.

Clearly, the situation will not develop as simply and smoothly as described above. There will probably be subgroups that continue unabated to meet the conditions described by Merry. One may think of people with highly traditionalist attitudes, or of those in highly dependent positions who continue to live in close-knit local communities. It goes without saying that the growing possibilities of shaping one's own life will not be taken up by everyone. These possibilities may hold a great attraction, but they can also present a certain threat. After all, people striving for autonomy do not know what the final outcome will be; there may thus be gains, but what about the losses? With regard to such questions, Bartels (1989: 316) tellingly refers to exploring a 'psy-cho-cultural *terra incognita*'.

Nor can one be certain about the economic and social conditions affecting individual choices. One may think of stagnating or even wors-ening unemployment among Turks, of increasing discrimination, or of a growing influence from conservative Muslim of nationalist groups. One needs also to consider the fact that many Turkish youngsters who grew up in the Netherlands have married partners raised in Turkey. Few of these factors, however, will be able to undo the developments that have begun to take place, and the process is, I believe, irreversible.[14]

Conclusion

This chapter has examined the role of gossip among Turks in the Nether-lands and has focused on girls and young women. Gossip has a negative effect on many girls' freedom of action, and sometimes even on their participation in school activities or the mere continuation of school attendance. Most of the girls detest this aspect of gossip and would like to have greater personal freedom. Yet although the girls describe the restrictions and the rigid social control resulting from them as 'typically Turkish', they wish to consider themselves to be Turkish, too. Their objections may result in an internal self-differentiation from their gossip-ing compatriots, but this never implies any desire to cease to be Turkish or embrace 'Dutchification' (*vernederlandsing*).

Yet I have also mentioned the first beginnings of change. Strict social control is no longer taken for granted, and it can even result in counter-productive effects because it no longer has the power to enforce con-formity. This implies a certain distancing from the group. As Bartels puts it (1989: 458), 'to perceive the collectivity in a negative light has thus become in itself an important step towards individual emancipation.' And he goes on to say: 'Of course, the image shift is also a[n as] yet mostly unconscious endorsement of the Dutch value system and there-fore clears the road to integration.' I shall not attempt to make predic-tions concerning integration and the nature of changes in the self-definition of Turkish girls, but one conclusion seems unavoidable:

their attempt to acquire the freedom so greatly desired goes hand in
hand with a redefinition of their Turkish identity. Whether this identity
will still be emphasized and recognized as Turkish in the long run, is an
open question.

Notes

1. My field research, conducted in 1984 and 1985, relied upon twenty-five Turkish
    girls and young women aged between 16 and 25. Its central interest was in the
    informants' experiential world and orientations. The informants were selected
    at random from the population register held by the city council of Amsterdam
    (15 people) as well as from the register of a smaller place (10 people). For a
    detailed report of the research see de Vries 1987 and 1990.

2. Social control includes both formal and informal processes. Cachet (1990: 51)
    points out that the two are seldom rigorously distinguished and makes an
    attempt at this (pp. 51-5). Reading (1977: 49) considers the most important
    distinguishing criterion to be the institutionalized mechanisms of formal social
    control as opposed to the non-institutionalized nature of informal social control.
    According to these and other definitions, gossip is preeminently a type of
    informal social control. In this paper I shall use the term 'social control' to mean
    informal social control only.

3. Other elements reported to be important for a Turkish cultural identity included
    norms about relations with others. Parents and older people should be treated
    more respectfully, and the opposite sex with greater reserve, than was thought
    the case among Dutch people. Emphasis was given also to a sense of continuity
    evidenced in connections with ancestors, traditions, customs and history (de
    Vries 1987: 177-8).

4. This distinction does not imply, of course, that Turkish girls who are gossiped
    about would never gossip themselves; they do.

5. The list can of course be extended. It would be interesting to consider especially
    those groups of migrants whose gossip does not have such pervasive effects
    upon girls. This is probably the case among Creole Surinamese in the Nether-
    lands. For further discussion see de Vries 1990: 26-8.

6. See Hannerz 1967: 45; Merry 1984: 277; Sabini and Silver 1978: 121.

7. Gluckman mentions this possibility almost as an aside. Once a process of
    disintegration has begun within a group, then even according to Gluckman
    (1963: 314), gossip and scandal will not counteract this, but rather speed up
    the process. However, he scarcely illustrates this possibility. Furthermore his

remark sounds somewhat curious, following a long exposition bristling with examples of the positive functions of gossip as a group-integrating and stabilizing factor.

8. A vivid picture of just such an ambivalence is given by van Stolk and Wouters (1984). It is instanced by a quite different group, Dutch married women who have run away from their husbands as a result of abuse.

9. The subject presents a classic case, of course, of the difficulties in distinguishing between ideology and practice. Danz et al. (1993), who have used quantitative methods to research sexual practices among Turkish, Moroccan, and native Dutch adolescents, received considerable numbers of replies that were incomplete or unreliable. Given these limitations, they conclude that among their Turkish female sample, it is some ten percent who are no longer virgins, comparing this to some 22 percent of their native Dutch sample. Girls with no sexual experience made for between 48 and 57 percent of the Turkish sample, contrasted with some 29 to 31 percent of the native Dutch sample. The remaining percentage of the latter had had some sexual experience excluding intercourse.

10. See Brouwer et al. 1992: 25-35, and de Vries 1987.

11. See Elias and Scotson 1985: 128-144; Hannerz 1967; Merry 1984.

12. See Risvanoğlu-Bilgin et al. 1986: 79; van Eekert and Gelderloos 1990: 119; de Vries 1987.

13. During the first period of their residence in the Netherlands (1951-ca.1960) Moluccans were housed in camps that were situated in relative isolation from Dutch citizen towns. During the 1960s many began to move into so-called 'open neighbourhoods'. Some then sought accommodation also outside these neighbourhoods. In 1978, about 22 per cent of the Moluccan population in the Netherlands lived outside a special neighbourhood or camp. By 1989, this figure had risen to about 60 per cent (Bartels 1989: 366).

14. It may be thought that I present too rosy a picture of the current situation. At present there is little sign of improvement in the socio-economic position of young Turks. Their educational profile is far from high, and unemployment among them is alarmingly high. To counter this, I would reiterate that I do not predict spectacular changes but do foresee increasing differentiation. An improvement of the educational level of the post-migration cohort has already been established, as mentioned above.

References

Bartels, D.
1989   *Moluccans in Exile. A struggle for ethnic survival*. Leiden: COMT, publ.
          nr. 32.

Bergmann, J.R.
1987   *Klatsch: Zur Sozialform der diskreten Indiskretion*. Berlin/New York: W. de
          Gruyter.

Böcker, A.
1986   *Netwerken en migratie: sociale netwerken en conjugale relaties van Turkse
          migrantenechtparen in Utrecht*. (M.A. thesis). Groningen: Instituut voor
          Culturele Antropologie.

Böcker, A.
1994   Op weg naar een beter bestaan. De ontwikkeling van de maatschappelijke
          positie van Turken in Nederland. In: H. Vermeulen and R. Penninx (eds.),
          *Het democratisch ongeduld. De emancipatie en integratie van zes doel-
          groepen van het minderhedenbeleid*. Amsterdam: 't Spinhuis

Brouwer, L., B. Lalmahomed and H. Josias
1992   *Andere tijden, andere meiden. Een onderzoek naar het weglopen van Ma-
          rokkaanse, Turkse, Hindostaanse en Creoolse meisjes*. Utrecht: Jan van
          Arkel.

Cachet, A.
1990   *Politie en sociale controle*. Arnhem: Gouda Quint.

Danz, M.J., T. Vogels and R.W.M. Gründemann
1993   *Jeugd en seks: kennis, houding en gedrag bij Turkse en Marokkaanse
          jongeren in Nederland*. Leiden: NIPG-TNO.

Doorn, J.A.A. van and C.J. Lammers
1969   *Moderne sociologie. Systematiek en analyse*. Aula-boeken 29. Utrecht/Ant-
          werp: Het Spectrum.

Eekert, P. van and E. Gelderloos
1990   *Vroeger was de wereld groter. Reacties op langdurige werkloosheid bij Tur-
          ken, Marokkanen en Surinamers*. Utrecht: Jan van Arkel.

Elias, N. and J.L. Scotson
1985   *De gevestigden en de buitenstaanders, een studie van de spanningen en
          machtsverhoudingen tussen twee arbeidersbuurten*. The Hague: Ruward.

Gluckman, M.
1963   Gossip and scandal. *Current anthropology* 4: 307-316.

Gluckman, M.
1986   Psychological, sociological and anthropological explanations of witchcraft and gossip: a clarification. *Man (N.S)* 3: 20-34.

Graafsma, T. and J. Tieken
1987   Leven in een 'condición migrante'. In: P.A.Q.M. Lamers (ed.), *Hulpverlening aan migranten. De confrontatie van culturen in de geestelijke gezondheidszorg*. Alphen aan den Rijn/Brussels: Samsom Stafleu, pp. 26-34.

Hannerz, U.
1967   Gossip, networks and culture in a black American ghetto. *Ethnos* 32: 35-60.

Merry, S.E.
1984   Rethinking gossip and scandal. In: D. Black (ed.), *Toward a general theory of social control. Volume 1: Fundamentals*. London: Academic Press, pp. 271-302.

Mungra, G.
1990   Hindoestaanse gezinnen in Nederland. Leiden: COMT.

Önen, E.
1989   *Het Turkse schoolcontactwerk in het voortgezet onderwijs in Zaandam. Periode 1986-1988*. Zaandam.

Reading, H.F.
1977   *A dictionary of the social sciences*. London: Henley/ Boston: Routledge and Kegan Paul.

Risvanoğlu-Bilgin, S., L. Brouwer and M. Priester
1986   *Verschillend als de vingers van een hand. Een onderzoek naar het integratieproces van Turkse gezinnen in Nederland*. Leiden: COMT (uitgave 24).

Sabini, J.P. and M. Silver
1978   Moral reproach and moral action. *Journal for the Theory of Social Behavior* 8: 103-123.

Stirling, R.B.
1956   Some psychological mechanisms operative in gossip. *Social Forces* 34: 262-267.

Stolk, B. van and C. Wouters
1983   *Vrouwen in tweestrijd. Tussen thuis en tehuis*. Deventer: van Loghum Slaterus.

Vries, M. de
1987   *Ogen in je rug. Turkse meisjes en jonge vrouwen in Nederland*. Alphen aan den Rijn/Brussels: Samsom.

Vries, M. de
1990   *Roddel nader beschouwd*. Leiden: COMT (publ. nr. 40).

Vries, M. de
  1993   Turkse meisjes in Nederland: de veranderende rol van roddel. *Migranten-
          studies* 1: 32-45.

Ware, C.F.
  1977   *Greenwich Village 1920-1930. A comment on American civilization in the
          Post-War Years.* New York: Octagon Books (reprint of 1935).

Wijk, N. van
  1985   *Ambon of Belanda? Een studie over Molukkers in Woerden, de enige ge-
          meente in Nederland waar Molukkers na opheffing van de plaatselijke
          kampen verspreid zijn gehuisvest.* Leiden: COMT (publ. nr. 19).

Part II

Commitments: not collective but cross-cutting

Disconnecting religion and ethnicity
Young Turkish Muslims in the Netherlands

Thijl Sunier

Introduction

(1) '... In fact there are three categories among Turkish youngsters in the Netherlands. The first are the "political people", they are occupied with blackening Turkey, the second are the ones who go to bars, and the third category you see here in front of you. The other two categories we call the people who went astray. They have been raised in a non-Islamic society and have been influenced by it. They have been left alone. They went to Dutch schools and were educated by Christian teachers. Such a teacher does not teach you that it is forbidden to look at other women or to do what animals do... It is our duty as Turks and Muslims to teach them that their lives are not on the street, but right here in the mosque... Already in Turkey I was afraid of going astray when I went to the town, but after migrating to the Netherlands I felt more attracted to Islam than ever. We as Turkish Muslims are being discriminated against by Dutch people. They consider us inferior. But we have the strength of our religion. We are not afraid, only of Allah. We have the greatest religion. With his belief one Turk can handle 50.000 Dutch. In Turkey Islam is very weak, unfortunately, but I think that we will bring real Islam to Turkey because of our experiences here.'

(2) '....A few years ago we moved to our present house. It is a neighbourhood where just a few Muslims live. Before that we lived in "South" [a neigborhood with a high percentage of migrants – TS]. In the beginning Dutch people looked very strange. They were not unfriendly, but a little bit aloof. But after some time we got acquainted with some of them. One day a lady went to the hospital. I think we were the only ones who went to her to bring her flowers, not even her Dutch neighbours visited her... Look, a real Muslim must build up good relations with his neighbours irrespective of their religion and wherever you are. I sometimes hear Muslims say that it is bad for our religion to

meet non-Muslims, nonsense!! I even think that by talking with non-Muslims you become a better Muslim. You can exchange ideas, and other people can see what real Islam is all about.

Many Muslims, especially those old people who are sitting in the tea-house the whole day, doing nothing except chatting... they have a very strange idea about Islam. They think that Islam is full of prescriptions which only a few people know exactly. They also think that the habits they brought with them from Turkey or Morocco are Islamic. They are constantly lamenting because they can never reach that level of knowledge. As a consequence they do nothing and close their eyes. This is not what Islam is all about. True, there is no real Islamic society in the world, but that does not mean that you can just wait for the things to come. You have to be active in everyday life. Allah gave us the principles of an Islamic society, but we Muslims have to make this society, either here or in Turkey or in any other place in the world. That is our responsibility..... It is true that there are a lot of prescriptions in Islam, but the extent to which you have to obey those rules is not prescribed. So for example many fathers force their daughters to wear the headscarf. Will that imply that she is a better Muslim then? I also think that wearing the scarf is an important prescription for women, but when a woman has a different opinion about it, you cannot change her opinion by forcing her. You have to convince her until she has the same opinion. Being Muslim is something which is in yourself.'

I recorded these contrasting statements during interviews with young adherents of Turkish Muslim organizations in the Netherlands. The striking differences between the two speakers do not lie so much in the importance of Islam or the religious conviction of each of the respondents. Both of them, let us call them Ahmet and Hasan, consider themselves convinced Muslims. Yet they represent two definitions of being Muslim, and one immediately notices that the criteria by which the boundary between Muslim and non-Muslim is constructed are very different in a variety of respects. They attach different meanings to Islam, emphasize different aspects, and draw different conclusions.

The interview with Ahmet took place in the early 1980s in the largest Turkish mosque in the city of Utrecht. The mosque is attached to the *Turkish Islamic Cultural Federation* .[1] Ahmet was a member of an informal youth association within the mosque. The interview with Hasan was conducted far more recently for my present research among members of Muslim organizations in the city of Rotterdam. Hasan is a member of *Milli Görüş*.[2] Both were twenty years old at the time of the interview.

One could treat these statements simply as two different ideologies which exist side by side among Turkish Muslims and thus reflect the range of the current ideological climate in Islamic circles. Although this is true to a certain extent, I consider the differences as two specific ways in which Islam is socially constructed within a specific given context. The reason why I chose two contrasting statements separated by a time span of twelve years is that they can help to illustrate how important contextual differences are in the process of identity construction.

Essentialism as an explanatory blind alley

Despite the huge amount of literature which has been published on Islam in Europe over the past fifteen years, the meanings attached to Islam are a topic neglected in most of the research. Migrants are in the first place approached as belonging to religious or cultural groups with more or less constant and clearly discernible features. Culture and religion can thus appear as if they were forms of 'baggage' taken from the country of origin and passed on unchanged and unreflected by socialization and enculturation. Members of a cultural group are thus thought to perceive themselves as different because they *are* different.

In this type of explanation, the fact that Muslims in the Netherlands and elsewhere in Europe organize themselves and go to mosques represents nothing more than religious continuity. Muslim organizations are the visible manifestations of the transmission and reproduction of culture and religion. There are Muslim organizations *because* there are Muslims.

Vermeulen (1992: 15-17) distinguishes four aspects of this so-called culturalist approach – a term coined by Bidney (1953). In the first place, the tendency to consider cultures as fixed and homogeneous units within clear-cut boundaries is most clearly shown in studies on the 'second generation' of migrants. They are assumed to live 'between two cultures' (eg. Saharso 1985), and 'culture' in such a context is equated with 'national' culture. A second aspect is the tendency to reify the culture concept, that is, to detach it from its makers and to attribute to it an autonomous status. A third aspect, and in my view the most fundamental, is the tendency to consider cultural continuity as the natural given, whereas change is considered problematic. Cultural change then implies a deviation from cultural essence.[3] A fourth characteristic is the tendency to consider culture as a residual explanation. This is done both by those who try to reduce culture to other factors, such as happens in Marxist approaches, and by those who attribute almost all behaviours of individual agents to culture. Culture can then be considered as that which generates action directly.

Culturalist or normative explanations thus take culture and religion as an explanatory phenomenon rather than a phenomenon which has to be explained. By considering culture as paramount to individuals, an implicit distinction is being drawn between 'cultural behaviour', and 'individual behaviour', and it is then just a small step to considering cultural behaviour as irrational. Yet, compliance with certain rules and obligations cannot be explained simply by referring to the fact that there *are* rules (Hechter 1983: 4). This would leave no room for what Hechter (1983: 6) calls an individual's 'choice-making discretion in all groups and societies'. To recognize this, the emphasis must be placed on understanding how individuals perceive and define their situation and how they act according to those perceptions.

The subject at stake in this chapter is a particular kind of 'choice-making discretion', namely the significance that individuals attach to religious and cultural symbols in explaining their present situation. Eickelmann (1987) has characterized the study of the relation between religious principles and societal context as 'a political economy of meaning'. 'A political economy of meaning contrives to achieve a balance between concern with the communication and the development of complex belief systems and how these systems shape and in turn are shaped by configurations of political domination and economic relations among groups and classes in societies of different levels of complexity' (Eickelmann 1987: 16). Other authors have also pointed to this change of meaning (eg. Schiffauer 1988). Islam thus has a different meaning for a Muslim who just arrived in Europe, than for somebody who has lived here for some time, and Islam means something different again to a Muslim with a low education and a poorly paid job than, say, for an academic. Such a personal construction of meaning is thus very much related to one's knowledge about Islam on the one hand, and to one's experiential knowledge and self-knowledge on the other.

These general considerations are all the more useful if, as in the statements presented, there are both religious and national categories involved in the construction of ethnic boundaries. The two cases illustrate well how it is two important markers of ethnic identity, Turkishness and Islam, that are related to each other. I will discuss the circumstances under which such identity constructions take place by presenting a contextualized portrait of both Ahmet and Hasan and will first describe their differing ideas about Islam and Turkishness, religious principles and Dutch society. I will then concentrate on the complex interaction of personal, societal and Islamic characteristics as they come together in the two cases.

Differences in the meaning of Islam and Turkishness

Islam and Turkishness

According to Ahmet, the identities of 'being Muslim' and 'being Turkish' were so inseparable as to coincide. To be 'a real Turk' (*hakiki Türk*) and 'a good Muslim' (*iyi müslüman*) appeared to be one, and there were indications that even the converse was true. Thus even people who undoubtedly belong to the Islamic world, for example Arabs, proved to be unable to live according to the principles of Islam, and it was thus that some 500 years ago they had to pass on the leadership of the '*umma* to the Turks. On the other hand, he had a very definite opinion about Turks who did not live according to Islam anymore. Of course, he admitted that for a growing part of the younger generation adherence to Islam was no longer self-evident, but he explained this mainly as a stronger orientation towards western society and a loosening of their ties with the home country. Ahmet professed a very strong emotional bond with Turkey, and in many ways idealized the country. He considered love for the fatherland a moral duty for every good Muslim. Consequently, every Turk who forgets about his religion forgets about his home country. He considered this not only as an assault to Islam but also a betrayal of the Turkish people. Some members of the informal group to which Ahmet belonged went so far as to state that those who did not pay enough attention to religion could not be 'real Turks' (*hakiki Türk*). 'Muslim', according to Ahmet, is thus an exclusive category and Islam serves as a kind of Turkish ethnic ideology. Although he was very sad about the fact that so few people were acting as real Muslims and so many neglected their religious duties, he did not try to convince me that conversion to Islam would be good for me, too. He did not blame me for not being a Muslim. I belonged to the Christian world and this constituted an almost insurmountable categorical barrier.

According to the second respondent, Hasan, anyone, irrespective of his or her background, could be or become a good Muslim. He thus thought it 'complete nonsense' (*saçma*) to single out the Turks as a specific category in Islamic history. Consequently, every society could finally become an Islamic society, provided certain conditions had been fulfilled. Although the history of Islam was related to the history of specific countries and peoples, Islam itself was considered a universalist and inclusive religion. The message was directed toward every living soul, and there were no countries and no peoples for whom Islam could be more suitable or appropriate than for others. For Turks it is as difficult or as easy as for any other person to become a good Muslim. Every view of Islam as a kind of national ideology was an assault to the very nature and message of Islam itself.

Hasan did not try to convince me either about the positive influence of Islam, not because of lack of interest, but because any pressure on people was unislamic in his view. 'There is no pressure in Islam' (*Islam'da zorlama yok*) was a much-quoted phrase among the young people I spoke with in the organization. Hasan considered my interest in Islam an important first step, but thought that becoming Muslim was an individual process in which other people could only play a marginal role. It is good to get assistance in your personal road to Islam, but basically it is a process which must come out of yourself. Hasan put this as follows: 'It took me quite a while before I realized that all the things I learned about Islam were also addressed to me and concerned my way of living.'

Religious principles

Although both Ahmet and Hasan admitted that being Muslim is related
to certain behaviours and rules, for Ahmet these rules were unam-
biguous, as well as the very essence of Islam. Apart from the 'Turkish'
essence of Islam mentioned already, Ahmet considered the boundary
between Muslim and non-Muslim as fixed and defined by concrete
rules, based on the five pillars of faith which he learned from religious
teachers and his parents. In other words, the community of Muslims was
constituted by a system of religious principles and norms. It turned out
that Ahmet had very little knowledge about the more philosophical
aspects of Islam. In general, the 'why' behind certain regulations and the
circumstantial meaning of these regulations were almost completely
unknown to him.

Hasan, on the other hand, considered Islam as a rather abstract code.
He emphasized the personal responsibility of every Muslim, for it was
not the community that was crucial for personal behaviour, but the
judgement of God. Many times during the interview he pointed at his
heart as 'being Muslim is situated there'. Being Muslim was concerned
with a certain level of consciousness, rather than obedience to simple
rules. Speaking about the boundaries between Muslim and non-Muslim,
he constantly changed his opinion depending on the topic which was
at stake. Sometimes he said that it was just a matter of interpreting
everyday experiences from an Islamic perspective, at other times he said
it was a matter of accepting the spirit behind the Revelation. Hasan was
very critical about religious authorities: 'You always have to check yourself what somebody says, even when it is an '*alim* (religious authority)'.

Dutch society

With such contrasting notions of Islam, the two young men exemplified
important differences in their views of Dutch society at large. Both were
very critical about it, but their criticisms were directed at different aspects
of Dutch society. Ahmet pointed to specific perceived behaviours, and
all examples he gave constituted the opposite of Muslim behaviour. I
stress the word 'perceived' since Ahmet, who did not have any contact
with Dutch people apart from his superiors at his work, had very little
knowledge about daily life. His observations tended to start with the

phrase: 'I heard that....', and his main source of knowledge were fellow members of the organization, the *'imam* and other *'ulema*, and elderly Turks who were in the same position as he was. Ahmet sometimes produced very remarkable examples. He had heard that Dutch children were forced by their parents to eat pork and were stimulated to have sex as soon as possible, in order to master 'the practice'. He also heard that it was common for young people to have sexual intercourse in public places such as parks and beaches. He had numerous other examples which all denoted immoral behaviour. He told me that he was very sad because his father had bought a television.[4] Now all the European filth could creep into their livingroom, and even a good Muslim would be influenced by this. As I said before, Ahmet had no desire whatsoever to take part in native Dutch social life and projected a very strong 'us/them' dichotomy. In addition, he also tended to draw a line between what he called *'sosyetik'* (belonging to the high/urban society) and *'köylü'* (belonging to the simple but honest village community). The best Muslims could be found in the small villages where modern life had not yet penetrated.

Hasan, on the other hand, spoke about underlying societal structures, and sometimes his analysis resembled that of a Marxist critique. Not the people were wrong, but the system. He spoke about relations between the West and the Third World, about imperialism, about classes and economic relations, about racism, but also about prostitution and drug and alcohol abuse as the products of a non-Islamic societal structure. Being a Muslim could protect one from evil, but what was more important was that such structures be changed. His examples reflected his active participation in Dutch social life, because he was familiar with all the subtleties of the general image about Islam. After all, the greater part of his daily activities took place among native Dutch people.

Hasan, of course, knew people who shared Ahmet's views, especially elderly people, as he explained. Yet in his opinion they were very afraid of the society in which they lived. As a matter of fact, Hasan felt sorry for them. 'They think that a good Muslim must withdraw from society when it is not Islamic. This is a very stupid idea. It does not serve Islam at all'. Living according to certain prescriptions did not, to him, constitute the beginning of being Muslim, but one possible result.

Contextual differences

In explaining and analyzing the differences in meaning that Ahmet and
Hasan attach to Islam, one can usefully focus on three contextual fields.
The first is related to personal characteristics at the time, the second to
characteristics of Dutch society at the time, and the third is related to the
changing roles and positions of Muslim organizations. The reason why
I chose two cases with a chronological difference of almost twelve years
was, as I have said, that this allows for a historical appreciation of social
developments between the beginning of the 1980s and the early 1990s.
This does not imply, of course, that one could not find important differences in personal characteristics among individuals at either period.
With respect to the characteristics of Dutch society, as well as those of
Muslim organizations, however, the differences between the two
periods are highly relevant, and the historical differences and differences of meaning can thus throw light on each other.

Personal and cohort differences

An important difference between Ahmet and Hasan is their position in,
and their knowledge about, 'Dutch society' in the broadest sense of the
word, and the extent to which they interacted with native Dutch people.
One could consider these differences as typical cohort differences to a
fair extent. Ahmet did not speak Dutch apart from a few useful words.
At the time indeed, few young people of the same age spoke Dutch with
any ease. This was no surprise, of course, in a cohort that had come to
the Netherlands recently, although there were also quite a few Turkish
youth who had been here for longer than Ahmet. It had also to do with
the fact that their socio-economic position, as well as the kind of work
they tended to do, did simply not offer them much opportunity to
interact with native Dutch people. Those who wanted to, had to put
considerable effort into getting into contact on a personal basis. Although some of them had enjoyed a fairly good education in Turkey,
they had to accept work for which a knowledge of Dutch was not
necessary, such as cleaning jobs and factory labour. There, the majority
of their colleagues were migrants as well. In so far as they had contacts
with Dutch people, these were mainly superiors. In their everyday

experiences, they had to contend with a hierarchical structure along ethnic lines. Most of the boys did not have more than primary school and a few years of secondary school. They had come to the Netherlands for family reunions, usually not more than five or six years ago. Most of them came directly from their village or town of origin. At the time of the interviews, Ahmet had been in the Netherlands for four and a half years, arriving from a little town in the province of Kayseri. He had moved there just two years before, leaving the village of his birth together with his mother and two younger brothers. They had stayed in the house of a brother of Ahmet's father. In town, Ahmet had the opportunity to work in the shop of his uncle who was a deeply religious man. Ahmet soon found himself engaged in voluntary work in the local mosque, acting as an assistant of the '*imam*. Just before Dutch law would have made it impossible because of his age, his father brought him to the Netherlands in 1977. At first he thought it interesting to migrate to the Netherlands; but soon he blamed his father for bringing him to a place where he realized his opportunities were slim.

Other respondents of Ahmet's cohort told me that their parents decided to take them out of school and bring them to the Netherlands for reasons of personal safety. Towards the end of the 1970s, the atmosphere at secondary schools in Turkey was chaotic because of the civil war. In the years right before the coup-d'etat of September 1980, more than ten people were killed almost daily in clashes between left-wing and right-wing groups. As political disputes and even violence spread among students of secondary schools, the situation grew tense. One was forced to take sides in these disputes and clashes even if one did not want to, but ignoring it could be as risky as taking part in it. In Ahmet's time, a comparatively large proportion of the young people between seventeen and twenty-five who came to Europe had had such experiences. This implies that they had to break off their education in Turkey with all the consequences for their future position in the Netherlands. The number of people who came to the Netherlands at a very early age was comparatively small at that time.

In short, the situation of this cohort in the Netherlands resembles that of the labour migrant cohort in several ways. A low level of interaction with native Dutch society was the general pattern. Some of Ahmet's

peers whom I interviewed expressed regret about this; in the organization to which Ahmet belonged, however, such feelings were rare. As
most of them considered their stay in the Netherlands temporary, and
as most of them did not feel themselves part of Dutch society, knowing
Dutch and having contacts with Dutch people outside the working place
or the school was not something one needed to put great effort into.

Economic factors were crucial in this respect. Most Muslim migrants
found themselves in very weak socio-economic positions. As life
chances tended to fall together with their religious background, we can
speak of what Du Preez (1980: 78-110) called an 'identity trap'. Their
hesitant attitude towards native Dutch society and their strongly inward
orientation can be seen as a kind of survival strategy, because there were
indeed few other options available to them. Ahmet and his peers reacted
to this situation by dissociating themselves from 'Dutch society' and by
professing the ideal of returning. As Blaschke (1980) pointed out with
respect to the situation in Germany, in the face of discrimination and
bad socio-economic prospects, there was a tendency among Muslims to
develop a form of ethnic ideology opposed to German society, in which
Islam played an important role as part of their ethnic heritage. Ahmet
and his friends, likewise, had an explanation for their perceived isolated
position in which Islam and Turkishness played a central role.

The situation twelve years later was different in several regards.
Hasan, like many of his peers, had come to the Netherlands at an early
age. Arriving in 1978 at the age of six, he had had only one year of
primary schooling in Turkey. Once in the Netherlands, he could join
Dutch primary education fairly easily. So, although both Ahmet and
Hasan came to the Netherlands roughly at about the same time, their
starting positions were entirely different. Fifteen years later Hasan spoke
Dutch better than Turkish. He had a pronounced Rotterdam accent, and
from the words and phrases he used, one could immediately notice that
he had intensive contact with native Dutch peers. Hasan attended secondary school and is currently finishing a technical high school. He has
given some consideration to going to university afterwards. Although,
of course, not all of his peers have done so well, there was a comparatively high percentage of youths in his organization that continued their
education at secondary level.

Apart from these typical cohort differences, there is an important personal difference between Ahmet and Hasan that concerns their knowledge of Islam. For Ahmet, Islam tended to come down to a knowledge of rules and principles as put forward by religious authorities. Although he had worked as a volunteer in a local mosque, this did not give him the opportunity to study Islam by himself. His work entailed mainly practical assistance to the local '*imam*. Islam was interwoven with his socialization and the rules and prescriptions of the community to which he belonged. Compliance with Islamic principles was considered equal to the loyalty to his community. This may be one of the reasons why he was so critical towards fellow Turks who did not care about religious prospects: if one turns away from Islam, one turns away from one's own community.

Hasan, on the other hand, did not discover an interest in Islam before the age of seventeen. His interest grew while participating in gatherings with peers reading about and discussing Islam. He thus learned about Islam from a very different starting-point, namely one that asked how to deal with the religion in one's personal and social life and how to face and understand daily experiences as a Muslim. This gave him, not so much a factual knowledge about Islamic prescriptions and principles, as an effectively personalized framework within which he could deal with his life here and now.

Changing attitudes in the Dutch public sphere

Apart from the cohort and personal differences, the images of Islam in Dutch society have a crucial influence on the experiences of Muslims in the Netherlands. They may not determine entirely how Muslims perceive themselves as citizens, or rather non-citizens, in that society. They may, however, be considered an important normative constraint and thus contribute to the reconstruction of Muslim identities in the Dutch context. Let me briefly describe these changes that took place between Ahmet's time and Hasan's time, i.e. over the past ten to fifteen years. In the beginning of the 1980s, the Dutch government issued a report (1983) in which it took permanency of residence as a starting point. 'Integration' became the principal focus of government policies. It was defined as fully-fledged participation in the central sectors of Dutch society:

labour, housing, and education. At the same time, migrants were formally granted the fundamental right to live according to their own cultural background, as long as this did not inhibit the process of integration. In fact, culture and integration were in a sense ideologically constructed as each other's opposites. More cultural background meant less integration and vice versa. Another implication of these new policies was that migrants were now increasingly defined along cultural lines, and less along economic lines as had been the case during the 1970s.

At the same time, due to the sometimes dramatic events in the Islamic world, such as the revolution in Iran, the assassination of the Egyptian president Sadat and more recently the Rushdie affair, Turks, Moroccans and other migrants from Islamic countries were 'discovered' as Muslims. A new category emerged: 'Muslim migrants'. For the sake of policy, people of entirely different backgrounds were lumped together under the heading 'Muslim culture'. Gradually, the alleged special character of Islam became the principal explanatory factor, not only for the attitude of people from the Islamic world, but also for a variety of problems with which they were faced in the Netherlands. Due to the negative image of Islam, this was of course not very beneficial for the people concerned. After all, it implied that Islam and its adherents were constantly considered as a burden on the shoulders of Dutch society, as a category for which integration was still far away.

In the same year in which this report was issued, the Dutch parliament also approved an important change in the Constitution. Henceforth, *all* religions were guaranteed equal rights in their relations with the central and the local state. Muslims succeeded in convincing policy makers, administrators and social workers that Islamic institutions, such as mosques and Islamic schools, constituted an important prerequisite to living according to the principles of their faith. In fact, according to at least some of the policy makers, Muslim organizations were the most important forms of organization among migrants. Many official documents emphasized the important social and psychological function of mosques and other institutions. Thus, despite the negative image of Islam, the emphasis on religious aspects, together with the constitutional changes, also created new opportunities for Muslims.

Turning from the governmental to a more general perspective, there are two types of political discourse with respect to the image of Islam and the position of Muslims in Dutch society. On the one hand, there is an image of Islam as a violent and repressive religion, in which Muslims are perceived of as rather intolerant religious fanatics ready to defend their religion by violent means. This image is reproduced time and again in the media and gained momentum during the Rushdie affair.[5] On the other hand there is an image in which Muslims are portrayed as pitiful, marginal creatures, not capable of climbing on the bandwagon of modernity and progress. Every manifestation of their presence *as Muslims* in Dutch society is considered as a proof of unfinished and even failed integration. It is especially this latter image which to a large extent underpins the policies towards Muslims.

It is largely as a consequence of this image that many young Muslims take pains to show it as a distortion which has to be corrected. Hasan's statement is a good example of this effort. He constantly referred to the fact that being Muslim does not imply that one has to turn away from the society one is living in. On the contrary, Islam gives one the strength to cope with everyday life as a full citizen. Ahmet, on the other hand, also considers Islam as an important source of strength, but one to dissociate himself from native Dutch society. This had not so much to do with the image of Islam, however, as with the deplorable economic situation in which he found himself.

The role of Muslim organizations

In the course of the 1980s, momentous structural, ideological and political changes both in Turkey and in Europe turned Islam into an important organizational principle. In the Netherlands, it has become the most important basis for organizational activity (Landman 1992), and especially youth organizations are growing rapidly.

Both Ahmet and Hasan emphasized that their commitment to Islam was a personal choice, but when we examine how they joined their respective organizations, there are again striking differences. After his arrival in the Netherlands, Ahmet almost immediately went to the mosque. Looking for the near-by mosque was in fact the first thing he did after his arrival. In this way, he continued to do what he did in Turkey where he had been an active volunteer in the local mosque. In the Dutch mosque, too, he soon met peers who became an important point of reference. At that time there was no youth organization with a separate room. The peer group to which Ahmet belonged was loose and informal. He told me that they used to listen to cassettes with important sermons and together discussed the contents. These cassettes and discussions appeared to me to influence much of what he said in the interviews, and although he tended to emphasize his personal experiences in Dutch society, these seemed to me to play a minor role.

His own relation to Turkey, like that of other people in the organization, showed an important difference when compared to the present situation. Ahmet had spent a great deal of his life in Turkey, but after migration he could only afford the opportunity to visit Turkey once. It was thus his memories that formed the most important point of reference. There was, furthermore, no Turkish television in the Netherlands at that time, although this has meanwhile become an important source of knowledge and information. The policy of the *Diyanet* to which the mosque subscribed was oriented towards keeping the communication channels to Turkey open and to preach love for the motherland. Not surprisingly these factors contributed to a somewhat unrealistic and idealized image of Turkey which could not be counterbalanced by recent personal experiences.

Hasan's way to the organization was different, and it had in fact very little to do with Islam. After migrating to the Netherlands, his father sent him to a Qur'an course, but when he went to secondary school he did not have the opportunity, nor the desire, to attend the mosque very often. As he felt he had other things to care about, Islam gradually became a minor factor in his life. He had joined the present youth organization only three years before I met him, but even then not because of any heightened Muslim commitment. In fact the main reason for his step was that he had become a member of the organization's football team. It was a friend who had introduced him to this, largely autonomous, club, and by meeting other people he gradually got involved in the youth organization itself. He admitted that his interest in Islam developed only after joining. Although he came to spend much of his time there, he also maintained lively personal contacts outside. Besides his schoolmates, he met other native Dutch peers on a variety of occasions. Although the policy of the youth branch of *Milli Görüş* is mainly oriented towards building up the internal structure of the organization, most of the present-day young male members interact intensively with Dutch society in a variety of situations. For most of them, the youth organization functions as an alternative to tea-houses and community centres, and the leadership itself spends far more energy on creating an atmosphere that suits young people than on teaching Islamic principles. There were indeed occasional tensions between the youth organization and the administrative board of the mosque next door. Influential persons in the mosque had doubts about activities like sports and watching video, as they considered these did not belong with a religious organization.

With respect to Turkey, Hasan takes a very different attitude from Ahmet's. For him, Turkey is a country he only knows from holidays. To put it strongly, going back to Turkey is as senseless as going to any other country. In general there was a very critical attitude towards Turkey in the organization to which Hasan belonged. *Milli Görüş* in Europe certainly does not stimulate something like uncritical love for Turkey, and it does not base its political commitments upon a specifically Turkish vision of Muslim politics. Hasan in his own way reproduced this discourse during the interview.

In Ahmet's 'days', one could predict that someone like Hasan would not engage in Muslim organizations, because there were no proper channels and means to attract somebody like him. Almost all the existing Muslim organizations were in their initial phases, and they had not yet developed a specific strategy oriented towards young people. Most of the mosques might have a small tea-house, but besides that there were few activities apart from religious services. The organizations had no experience in attracting young people. Had one predicted then that ten years later one would find pooltables, video facilities, football clubs and theater groups in Muslim organizations, they would certainly have greeted the idea with stunned disbelief. Ahmet and most of his peers in the organization did not, in fact, *become* members of the organization, so much as form part of it right from the beginning. At that time, young people tended to join the organization as part of pre-existing social networks, rather than by individual acts of personal commitment. In the early 1980s I also interviewed youngsters with characteristics more similar to Hasan's. Although they were certainly not negative about Islam, they thought of the Muslim organizations then existing as conservative and reactionary. In general they considered people frequenting Muslim organizations malintegrated village people. For them, Muslim organizations were too dependent upon the 'village culture' of recently migrated Turks. Despite their vague, though not negative, attitude towards Islam, identifying with these people was not a viable option for them, and nor did the virulent nationalism appeal to them. Rather they wanted to distinguish between 'rural' Turks and 'modern' Turks, and, identifying with the latter, wished to consider Islam and Turkish culture as two separate entities. They indeed blamed the 'new' immigrants for the negative images that Dutch people formed and with which they themselves were confronted. In fact, the identification of Islam with conservative 'village culture' was also the dominant image of Dutch people.

Conclusions

In conclusion, we need to relate the two young men's statements both to the difference in personal backgrounds and the contextual differences between the beginning of the 1980s and the beginning of the 1990s. This relation, however, can only be understood if we treat all the above-mentioned factors as mutually related to each other. As we saw, Islamic ideology as put forward by Ahmet and his peers was not at all oriented towards Dutch society. If one chose for Islam one chose against, or at least not for, Dutch society.

For Hasan, adherence to Islam had nothing to do with negative feelings towards Dutch society. It certainly did not serve as a survival strategy. He could get along very well without being a member of an Muslim organization and could easily consider himself a Muslim without identifying with Turkish village culture. Forming part of Dutch society was not an antithesis to being a Muslim. Appeals to the Turkish background of potential members has indeed become a less and less necessary part of the ideology of Muslim organizations. On the contrary, according to some of the leadership of *Milli Görüş*, this appeal to Turkish identity might in some cases be counterproductive. Most of Hasan's peers share his attitudes towards Turkey and an Islam that is not predicated on national identities. Although his Turkish background was beyond question it was at the same time no issue. It did not play an important role in the way in which he defined his being Muslim. His Turkish background was self-evident, but not more than that. Many times he stated: "of course I am Turkish, but.....". To consider oneself a part of Dutch society despite holding very critical opinions about the principles of that society and despite one's commitment to Islam has become quite common over the past decade or so. There are simply more identity options available now than there were ten years ago. I therefore conclude that there is a tendency observable among at least a part of young Turkish Muslims in the Netherlands ideologically to detach their religious from their national identifications.

Notes

1. TICF is an umbrella organization founded by supporters of the so-called 'official' Islam as recognized by Turkish state authorities. Since the founding of the Turkish Republic in 1923, Islamic institutions such as mosques, Qur'an schools and educational centres for religious personnel have been formally subsumed under state control. These institutions are run by the 'Directorate of Religious Affairs (*Diyanet*). Imams are employees of the state. Dutch and other European mosques which belong to this umbrella organization have their imams sent over and paid for by the Turkish state. Other mosque organizations have to pay their imams themselves.

2. *Milli Görüş* is an umbrella organization founded by supporters of the Turkish *Refah Partisi* ('Welfare Party') which is the only legal Islamic political party in Turkey, and considered 'fundamentalist' by its opponents. The political movement is very critical towards state control of religion and religious institutions. In Europe, *Milli Görüş* is especially successful among young people.

3. See also J. and J. Comaroff (1992). In studies on Islam essentialism is widespread. For a discussion see Sunier and Termeulen (1991) and Zubaida (1988).

4. At that time there were no Islamic broadcasting companies yet and no direct connections with Turkish state television. The only programmes they could receive were European ones.

5. Shadid and van Koningsveld (1992); Haleber (1989).

References

Bidney, D.
    1953   *Theoretical Anthropology.* New York: Columbia University Press.

Blaschke, J. & K. Greussing (eds.)
    1980   *'Dritte Welt' in Europa: Probleme der Arbeitsmigration.* Frankfurt am Main: Syndikat.

Du Preez, P.
    1980   *The Politics of Identity. Identity and the Human Image.* Oxford: Blackwell.

Eickelmann, D. F.
    1987   Changing Interpretations of Islamic Movements. In: Roff, W.R. (ed.), *Islam and the Political Economy of Meaning. Comparative Studies of Muslim Discourse.* Berkeley: University of California Press, pp. 13-31.

Haleber, R. (ed.)
    1989   *Rushdie-effecten. Afwijzing van moslimidentiteit in Nederland.* Amsterdam: SUA.

Hechter, M. (ed.)
    1983   *The Microfoundations of Macrosociology.* Philadelphia: Temple University Press.

Landman, N.
    1992   *Van Mat tot Minaret. De institutionalisering van de islam in Nederland.* Amsterdam: VU-uitgeverij.

Minderhedennota
    1983   *Minderhedennota.* Den Haag: Tweede Kamer.

Roff, W. R.
    1987   Introduction. In: Roff, W.R. (ed.), *Islam and the Political Economy of Meaning. Comparative Studies of Muslim Discourse.* Berkeley: University of California Press, pp. 1-10.

Saharso, S.
    1985   De tweede generatie: (voor eeuwig) verloren tussen twee culturen? *Psychologie en Maatschappij* 32: 371-385.

Schiffauer, W.
    1988   Migration and Religiousness. In: Gerholm, T. & Y. G. Lithman (eds.), *The New Islamic Presence in Western Europe.* London: Mansell Publishing, pp. 146-159.

Schwartz, T.
    1978   Where is culture? Personality as the distributive locus of culture. In: Spindler, G.D. (ed.), *The Making of Psychological Anthropology.* Berkeley: University of California Press, pp. 419-441.

Shadid, W.A.R. and P.S. van Koningsveld
1992   *De mythe van het islamitische gevaar. Hindernissen bij integratie.* Kampen: Uitgeversmaatschappij J.H. Kok.

Sunier, T. en A.J. Termeulen
1991   Islamisme als tegenideologie. In: Boele van Hensbroek, P., S. Koenis & P. Westerman (eds.), *Naar de Letter. Beschouwingen over fundamentalisme.* Utrecht: Grafiet, pp. 163-185.

Vermeulen, H.
1984   *Etnische Groepen en Grenzen.* Weesp: Wereldvenster.

Vermeulen, H.
1992   De cultura. Een verhandeling over het cultuurbegrip in de studie van allochtone groepen. *Migrantenstudies* 8, 2: 14-31.

Zubaida, S.
1988   *Islam, the People and the State.* London: Routledge.

The predicament of mixing 'culture' and 'religion'
Turkish and Muslim commitments in post-migration Germany[1]

Lale Yalçın-Heckmann

The Turks in Germany, including the first generation labour migrants and their children and grandchildren who were mostly born in Germany, compose the largest group among Germany's foreign population. A very high percentage of these Turks, who are internally differentiated into various sub-groups, such as Kurds, Laz, and Alevis, are Muslims and maintain a Muslim identity with varying shades of commitment. When I interviewed a Turkish migrant woman who had been living in Nürnberg over a period of fifteen years, she expressed her experiences of being a devout Muslim among the German Christians with the following words:

'I see that those who call themselves Christians today fulfill their religious duties by going to church on Saturdays and Sundays. This they do even if their religion is superstitious (*batıl*) and misled. After having seen these things, I have found them myself. This is what they believe in. For instance, we have just had their religious holidays.[2] They talk about our Prophet Isa, [the Muslim word for Jesus, LY], peace be upon him, as if he would descend on a pine tree, or as if he would ascend to heaven.. [Yet] they perform these rituals so well. I went around to observe the people around me and saw a great commotion in the Christian world. I have seen this everywhere, from shopping centers to the banks. I went especially to the bank – as I always get our money on the day it arrives there, so that it cannot to be used for interest rates. Even there, in a corner of the bank, they had put up a huge pine tree, all decorated with objects. Believing that our Prophet Isa will descend there, they decorated it with religious symbols, such as sheep and lambs and similar objects. There I have seen how they try to spread their religion, even to the banks, with the use of these symbols. I witnessed this myself. We have learned these things anyway in the last fifteen years. And when I think about it, I find it horrible that for New Year's Eve, 165 million Marks were spent on fireworks...'

The woman should not be seen as being a 'typical' example of Turkish Muslimhood in Germany. Rather, she belongs to a radical camp[3] and claims to lead a politically conscious life first as a Muslim and then as a Turk. Nevertheless, the passage demonstrates various themes in the negotiation of commitments among the migrants in post-migration Germany. To begin with, she perceives the Germans, or rather the Bavarian Germans around her, as being essentially religious, and she approves of this. Secondly, practising and living according to a religion is seen as a desirable trait, even if the Christian religion, especially after the Reformation, has been misled. So her preference is definitely for people living and practising the religions of the Book, i.e. Christianity, Judaism and Islam, instead of being atheists or agnostics. Within this second theme, it is even possible to discern her readiness for accepting religious pluralism, although she would probably defend the supremacy of Islam and insist on her right to criticize others for not seeing that 'they have been misled.'[4] Thirdly, she classifies the period of Advent, Christmas and New Year's Eve as one continuum of religious holidays and makes hardly any differentiation between the religious and secular significances attached to them by Germans. Fourthly, she alludes to a version of the story of the Christmas tree which I have heard a few times during my research. It attempts, on the one hand, to find a functional explanation for the Christmas tree, but on the other hand, its illogical structure casts an element of humour and perhaps ridicule upon the practice. The story is based on an imputed linguistic misunderstanding: the reason why Germans decorate a Christmas tree is that they have 'misunderstood' the word *Şam* (Turkish for 'Damascus' in Syria) for the word *çam* (Turkish for 'pine tree'). According to an underlying mythical story, the prophet Isa, who is supposed to descend to Earth as a messiah (*mesih*), will appear in Damaskus and ride on a white horse tied in front of the great mosque (*Masjid-i Aqsa*). It is with this expectation, allegedly, that a white horse is indeed tied up, every Friday, outside this mosque. The point of the story is that the Germans 'misunderstood' the word *Şam* (Damaskus) to mean *çam* (pine tree), which is why they decorate a pine tree (*çam*) every year, expecting their Prophet to descend upon it.[5] The woman who alluded to the story took it seriously enough and used it to support her arguments on how 'misled' Christianity was. A fifth theme

of the excerpt relates to the confidence she places in her knowledge of
Christianity in Germany. She often underlines that she looks for, ob-
serves, and tries to identify the religious practices and traditions around
her. Hence the consumerism of Christmas (Miller 1993) is secondary to
its religious effectiveness. For her, the season's consumerist activities are
to be understood as a 'religious commotion and activity in the Christian
world.' Following from this theme, a sixth point may emphasize the
overall presence of Christianity and the woman's perception of its per-
vasive power. Even the banks are seen to propagate religion. Finally,
the time factor in her perception is significant. She has been observing
and living in this society for the past fifteen years; she knows it. In fact,
she follows the media reports on the extravagant cost of New Year's Eve
fireworks. At the same time, however, she would not recognize the
Christian Churches as among the harshest critics of this expenditure,
even when I pointed this out to her.

The text quoted above should be read neither for its exotic flavour[6]
nor for its representativeness, but rather for its quality of illustrating
certain processes of negotiating one's own and other religious and ethnic identities. Minorities in post-migration Germany individually and
collectively observe, classify, negotiate and contextually hybridize elements of 'their' and of the 'others'' cultures and religions. Amidst these
individual and collective processes, there arise tensions concerning the
boundaries of cultures and religions; tensions about how, and by whom,
these boundaries should be defined; and tensions about whether and
why these boundaries may be effective. This chapter will discuss the
causes and forms of these tensions as well as the negotiations which aim
at resolving them. Ethnographically it focuses on Turkishness and Muslimhood in post-migration Germany, and on how these diacritica are
combined by Turks, Muslims and Germans to negotiate their boundaries
of individual and collective identity.

The complex processes of assimilation and resistance to assimilation
in the history of labour migration do not only produce postmodern
cultural expressions and collages of symbols, but they also lead to emotional debates about the 'authenticity' or 'mix' of traditions. These debates are conducted by cultural actors, interlocutors, analysts, and outside obervers. Social scientific studies of migrants and their adaptation

processes have produced various authoritative diagnoses which have subsequently been adopted by 'cultural practitioners'. In Germany, these are usually referred to as *Multiplikatoren,* a term used for both foreign and German persons who culturally or socially interact with the migrants and their offspring, and who range from social and community workers to ethnic artists and businessmen. In these depictions, the 'culture' of Turkish migrants is described by terms such as 'traditional' or 'Islamic' and is focussed on the first generation of migrants. The second generation's cultural identity is described by terms such as 'in-between', or with metaphors such as 'between two chairs' (*zwischen zwei Stühlen*) or 'between two worlds' (*zwischen zwei Welten*).[7] These ideas are used not only by social scientists and social workers who study or assist the post-migration community, but also by the migrants and post-migrants themselves (Lutz 1991: 230). Their own term for adaptation or assimilation is *uyum* (*Anpassung* in German), and the limits and forms of *uyum* are central to debates on Turkish identity and religion in post-migration Germany.

Syncretic processes have been recently problematized in writings on multiculturalism and religious pluralism (Stewart and Shaw 1994). Discussions about syncretism, however, have been largely missing in writings on the Islam of Turkish migrants. The Islamic religion of migrants has been discussed either within frameworks of modernity (Thomä-Venske 1981, Schiffauer 1991) or else within the context of political and religious movements and associations (Binswanger and Sipahioğlu 1988), embracing various types of Islam such as 'orthodox'/ urban versus rural Islam, which are thought to be transferred to the migrant and even to the post-migration setting. If there is any consideration of mixing different religious traditions at all, it has been sought between these various 'types' of Islam and Islamic practices. Hence, urban Islam becomes politicized and develops into a political-Islamic project led by religious organizations, or it is said that Alevi Islam adapts secularist Turkish republican discourse in order to construct and accommodate a new identity (Mandel 1989; Wilpert 1988).

If accepting, refuting, or ignoring syncretism in religion are ways of negotiating power on the part of various agencies (Stewart 1994), then the recognition of syncretism within the post-migration culture, and its refutation within the context of migrant Islam,[8] are issues which need to be explored. More specifically, it raises such problems as, who has the authority to define the authenticity of 'migrant Islam', how various groups and individuals within the migrant community deal with the question of *uyum* between various religious traditions, and where Turkish parents, for instance, draw the boundaries of religious mixing in rituals, festivals and other practices. Moreover, labour migrants from Turkey have differing views of religion, as will be discussed in the case of the headscarf below. Given this heterogeneity, do Turks in Germany show *uyum* in the domain of religion? If so, do they acknowledge it as such, or is 'migrant Islam' categorically closed to *uyum* in public but more negotiable in private, within the family or for the second generation? If the surrounding Christian German culture poses a challenge for Muslim rituals and their social significance and meaning, what sorts of processes take place in order to meet these challenges, and to what degree are these intentional? And if migrant parents are concerned with the influence of Christian traditions, where do they seek resolutions and where and how do they confront these influences? These are some of the questions which are significant in exploring syncretic practices and commitments and which may be articulated as cultural in some contexts but religious in others. In order to be able to talk about 'migrant Islam' and its multiplicity of contested meanings and practices, however, we should locate it briefly against the background of labour migration from Turkey and then the development of Islam within Turkey.

Turkish labour migration to Germany

As a governmental policy, Turkish labour migration to Germany began over thirty years ago and was stopped in 1973. Turkish migration since the 1960s can be roughly divided into three phases: first came male and female workers as individuals, recruited for certain jobs and living in workers' residence halls. The second phase was marked by the cessation of new labour recruitment, followed by the arrival of family members, husbands, wives and children. The third phase was reached with the third generation of migrants, or perhaps better post-migrants, born and living in Germany. Presently the Turks compose a community of nearly 1,9 million people, the largest category of foreigners in Germany. Foreigners altogether comprise ca. 7% of the total population. Although the Turkish population was predominantly working-class during the first two decades of migration, its occupational structure has undergone considerable changes. Thus, there are about 35,000 Turkish small businesses in Germany, creating jobs for over 125,000 people, and this trend is on the increase. Over 45,000 Turkish families have bought houses and property in Germany, strengthening the trend of becoming a permanent ethnic community and minority. With these slow but consistent changes in demographic structures and the penetration of Turks into almost all social strata within German society, – albeit without fundamental rights with regard to political representation due to their 'foreigner' (*Ausländer*) status – the Turkish community in Germany is becoming increasingly integrated into German political discourse, organized through local and nationwide associations,[9] and hence a social and political force to be reckoned with.

Turkish state and Turkish Islam

Very broadly surveyed, Islam within the Ottoman Empire was dominated by Sunni '*ulema* (doctors of Islamic law), who, on the one hand, denied any syncretic tendencies and mingling with unorthodox interpretations such as those of the Shia or the Alevi. Yet on the other hand, they did not totally control the everyday practice of 'folk Islam', which was partially led and sustained by religious orders (*turuq*).[10] Hence, orthodoxy was defined through a religious center which marginalized syncretic practices and interpretations of Islam.

The establishment of the Turkish Republic dealt a devastating blow to the center-periphery versions of Islam and to their coexistence. Republican ideology radically separated religion from state ideology, but in order to maintain this separation it tried, somewhat paradoxically, to organize 'orthodox' as well as 'unorthodox' Islam under the control of the state. The early republican period in particular was marked by ideological projects and studies on pre-Islamic customs, symbols, and folklore, with a consistent effort to underline the continuity between pre-Islamic and Islamic folk culture(s), redefined as the Anatolian culture(s), within the borders of the new republic.[11] Throughout the seventy years of Turkish republican social history, marked by the spread of mass education and urbanization, the ideology of the new elites incorporated visions and ideas of a pre-Islamic past, exemplified by the reification of the allegedly high status of women in the pre-Islamic Turkish tribes and states. These early republican efforts at rewriting the history of Turks with an emphasis on the virtues of pre-Islamic traditions have more recently become a target of critique for Islamic intellectuals (Meeker 1991).

The debates on the culture and meaning of Turkish Islam now current among the migrants in Germany are predicated on this general background, without necessarily re-introducing the historical issues in any explicit way. Nonetheless they appear imbedded in a dialogue with various sections of the population in Turkey, with political and religious movements in Turkey and beyond, and, last but not least, with German society. For it is the profession of Islam that is recognized as the most significant distinguishing characteristic of the Turkish post-migration community which defines them as 'other' both in their own definitions and in the eyes of the 'outsiders', the dominant German society (Elsas 1983, Thomä-Venske 1988). The twin features largely characteristic of the Islam of Turks in Germany are that it is urban, sometimes metropolitan, and closely linked to the media and its representations. Islamic media, after all, have been flourishing in Turkey, and many migrants are buyers of these journals, videotapes, and cassettes, which, among other subjects, treat Islamic history and politics. Nevertheless, the debate on modernity is not yet outdated within the Muslim discourse. Even though postmodernity allows for eclecticism, the resulting mixture of images is by no means collectively and smoothly accepted as the articulation of religious or popular pluralism. The debate on *uyum* is a case in point. *Uyum* is favoured by many migrants when it means adapting, for instance, to consumption patterns, work habits, or different notions of time-use. However, when it comes to *uyum* in religious practice, the degree of flexibility has to be carefully negotiated and contextualized. '*Herkesin dinî kendine*' ('each to [lit.: has] her/his own religion') summarizes the common concern for maintaining religious domains separate from one another. How to judge authenticity, how to interpret religious rules of commensality, how far certain 'new' celebrations are compatible with Islam – these are daily questions for many migrants. Pnina Werbner (1990) who studied the phenomenon of change in Islamic concepts and practices among Pakistanis in Manchester, suggests that ritual is 'naturalized' in the context of migration. The performance of Muslim sacrifices and offerings, for instance, presupposes the existence of a category of people who can be defined as 'the poor'. As this category is considered to be absent in the new local context, the migrants are induced to reflect on 'the taken-for-granted features of rites' (Werbner 1990: 154). Similarly to the Pakistani Muslims in Manchester, the Turkish Muslim migrants in Germany are compelled to be conscious of rites of commensality, ritual cleanliness and other religious tenets within the post-migration context. Likewise, they have to resolve the problem of reconstructing their 'community', to redefine the 'significant others' in ritual, and to cope with the 'problem of history and their particular part in it' (ibid: 1). Hence, how changes in religious ritual and meanings are to be interpreted is dependent on how migrants define their migration and post-migration experiences and their relationships to the receiving society. A highly significant marker of this shift in historical and symbolic belonging can be observed in burial rites, when migrants begin to bury their dead in the country of immigration instead of their 'home' country (ibid: 155). This trend is observable among the Turks in Germany as well. In this search for their place as Turkish Muslim migrants in German society, they re-shape many religious concepts and practices, albeit with marked ambivalences. An exemplary case can be seen in the interpretations of the 'sacred Christian time' that begins with Advent and extends to Christmas, the New Year, and Epiphany.

German Christmas and New year's eve

In Germany, as elsewhere in Europe, New Year is celebrated with festive firework displays that begin at midnight and last until the early morning. Young and old pour into the streets to let off their fireworks, spending hours outdoors and creating an atmosphere which is sometimes described as 'warlike'. On the following day, newspapers report not only on the glamour of the celebrations, but also on the enormous amounts of money 'blown into the air' – a point taken up in the earlier interview. Church groups complain that so much money should be wasted on displays that bring no moral or social benefits. These firework celebrations, however, are very popular with children, and parents find it difficult to refuse them what they enjoy so much. Children of Turkish labour migrants are no exception. A working-class Turkish father answered my question how the non-Muslim environment affected the upbringing of his children as follows:

> 'For instance, *Weihnachten* (Christmas) is a religious holiday; and those rockets, bombs [i.e. fireworks and firecrackers]... I actually buy those things for my children. Many people say that there's no such thing in our religion! All right, I *know* there's no such thing in our religion, but we don't have the ability to explain this to a seven-year-old child! Even if we had the ability to explain, the child can't understand it... When all other children are playing with fireworks and making lots of noise out on the street, how could you keep your child tied up indoors? That would give exactly the opposite impression, the opposite of what we desire. I am not encouraging my children to partici- pate in this, but when they want ten fireworks I buy five or six for them .. It is not only me; nobody could reason with a child when his friends are playing with fireworks on the street, telling him "look, we are Muslims"... He will then simply abhor Islam.'

Whether firework displays are compatible with Islam or not is a concern that Muslim Turkish parents face once a year. But shifting definitions of proper or improper behaviour among the younger generation, negotia- tions of flexible religious symbols and meanings, and the insecurity of reproducing or controlling these meanings are part and parcel of every- day life for Turkish Muslim post-migrants.

Many Turkish migrants conflate New Year's Eve with Christmas. Nevertheless, the meaning and form of Christmas celebrations is signi- ficant not only as illustrating the ways of negotiating Islamic religious symbols in the diaspora context, but also because its meaning for Chris- tian Germans is far from unitary. For many people in southern Germany, characterized by strong rural Catholic traditions, the period of Advent and Christmas represents a religious 'sacred time', although the 'sacred' elements may be latent and the cultural and social meaning of Advent and Christmas emphasized. It is also a period marked by a plethora of commercially marketed consumer goods. They range from Advent and Christmas decorations to goods such as candles, stars, lanterns, chocolates in the form of St. Nicholas and St. Martin, angels, pine wreaths (*Adventskranz*), wall-hangings and wooden figures. The colours white, silver, gold, green and red dominate almost all public spaces, be they shops, banks or offices, or the schools that are attended by Turkish children, too. Also private homes have their windows, doors and gardens decorated for Advent and Christmas. These decorations and products are introduced as early as the beginning of November and are not usually taken down before Epiphany on January 6. School and kindergarten children spend much time producing (*basteln*) various ornaments and pictures in which religious symbolism takes a central, albeit often unexplained, place.

Turkish children who attend German classes[12] take part in all these activities, as do younger Turkish children who engage in religiously oriented games, songs and crafts in community kindergartens run by the Protestant or Catholic Church. During my school visits around Christmas time, I saw Turkish children drawing pictures of the infant Jesus (*Christkind*) appearing at the '*Frauenkirche*' in the market square of Nürnberg, a place internationally known for its traditional Christmas market. Even those Turkish pupils who attended 'national classes' were surrounded by Advent and Christmas decorations in the classroom spaces they shared with 'German classes'.

How, then, are these symbols and practices, from Christmas decorations to religious songs and plays, perceived by, and incorporated into, the religious and cultural order of Turkish migrants? The behaviour and reasoning of the father cited above is typical in many ways: he chooses a practical strategy of 'accommodation within limits'. For him, the Christian religion and especially the Church are dominant and powerful presences, and their effects on Turkish children should be reckoned with and dealt with. Hence, practical strategies of accommodation are necessary, if one is to avoid overreaction from children. The father would probably not see this solution as religious syncretism, although he would define the confrontation and challenge as occurring between two religious, as opposed to cultural, domains.

To the ordinary German this example might raise rather different questions. Drawing on personal intuition and on discussions with friends and colleagues in Germany, I should suggest that there is a general consensus on the nature of German state and society, namely that they are basically secularized. Leaving aside the political and historical justifications for this claim, it is evident, nonetheless, that the realities of secularization are highly differentiated, especially when it comes to regional and traditional differences. The strongly Catholic areas of rural Bavaria or the Rhineland and Westphalia vary greatly from large cosmopolitan cities like Berlin or Hamburg. The Church also has different claims to power in different parts of the federation (*Bundesländer*), as exemplified by the larger number of religious holidays in traditionally Catholic states or the presence of crosses or crucifixes in classrooms in Bavaria. Nevertheless, it is commonly believed, and argued by the media, that religion has become a secondary issue, and that the Church – the Catholic even more than the Protestant – is steadily losing its influence. These claims sometimes refer to the number of people giving up their Church membership. Hence for many, the celebrations and paraphernalia related to Advent and Christmas appear mainly to be connected to German culture and local and regional traditions ('*ein Stück Heimat*'). Alternatively, they are considered a result of market forces and consumerism, and thus have even less to do with the 'essentials' of religion.

For many Germans, *Weihnachten* exhibits historically syncretic elements, as exemplified by the Christmas tree which is traced to originally 'heathen' Germanic custom. Furthermore, similar to other western and European Christmas celebrations, it is dominated by consumption-orientated and family-centered activities, and these focal concerns effectively overshadow the presence of religious symbolism (Miller 1993). Many of my friends indeed explained the presence of Christian symbols between Advent and Epiphany as a kind of 'survival' of religious and local/traditional customs (*Sitte*). Ritualistic activities that range from shopping through baking to decorating the Christmas tree are thus said to be performed mainly for children. At the same time, they may be explained as reenactments of one's own childhood *Weihnachten*, with its evocative smells, lights and tastes, but they are hardly ever validated as invocations of specifically religious symbols and meanings.

These contrasting views of the 'sacred' Christian time by Germans and Turks could be seen as a cultural misunderstanding in some ways; yet in others, they represent an effort to preserve the social markers of religious identity which are themselves ambivalent and multidimensional. Turkish parents tend to adopt or tolerate the adoption of consumerist behaviour related to Christian celebrations, and provide functionalist, pragmatic or aesthetic explanations of their behaviour. In contrast to the woman interviewee quoted at the outset, the father quoted later saw it as unavoidable to allow his son to play with fireworks on New Year's Eve, or to give presents to his teacher or friends on this occasion. He, like many other Muslims, would also support similar consumerist practices in a Muslim context, such as collectively giving children presents and celebrating the Muslim religious holidays with food and gift-giving within the mosque.

For some parents, on the other hand, the period of Advent and Christmas represents an unacceptable influence on their children, as the young unavoidably learn and perceive not only the visual Christian symbols but also Christian songs and prayers related to Advent and Christmas. A mother complained that her daughter kept singing these Christmas carols all day long and that she was unsure how to stop her daughter without hurting her feelings or being too harsh: 'These songs are actually prayers, they sing them in Church; so I tell her not to sing them *all* the time at least.' Yet other parents were hardly concerned about children's games and songs related to Advent and Christmas. While they knew that their children might have taken a role as the 'shepherd' or the 'sheep' in games enacting the story of the Nativity, they did not think that such participation in games with a religious context had any effect on their children. 'They are just children', said a mother, 'they do it as play, dressed up for Christmas as for carnival (*Fasching*)'.

Generational differences and islamic discourses

The need to interpret religious and cultural rites in a new environment is closely linked to the social history of labour migration. From the first generation of migrants onwards, processes of reconstructing the 'sacred' (*kutsal*) and the 'religious' (*dinî*) have come to show fundamental differences. To begin with, the two generations of Turks in Germany whom I have taken into consideration, have encountered religion and Islam in different ways.

Parents learned Islam and were socialized to become Muslims primarily in Turkey. Islam was mediated to them in different ways, depending on various factors: rural or urban background, the region of origin, the specific socio-economic standing of the family and the educational, professional and individual biography of each person. The variations ranged from strictly normative or official interpretations of Islam to mystical, notably Sufi influences, and from the highly secularist to the rigidly moralist. What was common to all parents of the first generation was, however, that they were all taught 'religion' as a subject in primary school for at least two years. Many parents I talked to in Nürnberg had grown up in villages or small towns where they had attended Koran courses taught by private persons or the *imam*.

A second common characteristic of the parental generation is their indirect religious socialization. The parents who later migrated to Germany had their religious knowledge mediated not only within the family or at school, but also through the larger community, media and institutions which shared and reproduced the common belief system. These indirect ways of mediating Islamic beliefs and values seem to be the most difficult to reproduce in the diaspora. Parents miss the influence of the larger social environment which articulates the Islamic idiom. A parent formulated this deficiency as follows: 'Here children can't live their religion fully; if they had been in Turkey, for instance, they would have heard the *ezan* (call to prayer) five times a day, and would at least have remembered [their] religion. But here, instead of *ezan*, they hear the church bells.'

In the diaspora, some of the Islamic prescriptions gain a particular weight and new meaning. One case in point is the practice of veiling, or rather covering the hair and the body in a particular style dictated by the Islamic fashion (*tesettür modası*). Although veiling has become a political issue and a potent symbol for Islamic revivalists and political activists in Turkey,[13] Turkish migrants in Germany regard the headscarf as an index of ethnic and gender identity in a foreign context. Yet, what it signifies is debatable among the migrants themselves. Many Turks in Germany see the headscarf as the anti-symbol of 'modernity', 'female emancipation', or 'willingness to integrate or assimilate' into the German society. For them, it represents not solely a symbol of pure religiosity, but a straightforward Islamic prescription. This interpretation of the headscarf, and the view that women with headscarves are identified as Turks, are widely known among the younger Turks. This inclination, however, contrasts with the issues of the headscarf debate as it is conducted in Turkey by various groups of intellectuals, feminists or urban-educated professional women. The rights and liberties won by women with the establishment of the Turkish Republic are being currently re-formulated and critically assessed by feminists of various persuasions (cf. Sirman 1989). Nevertheless, the belief in the need to defend these rights as the central value of the republican ideology remains deeply rooted among the educated classes. As these values are passionately contested by Islamic revivalists, the reasons for, and types of, covering the head are crucial for a classification of political views. In Germany, those women who do not wear a headscarf are widely seen as 'assimilated', 'Germanized Turks', or else as 'religiously liberal and modern Turks', as it is often formulated by or for Alevi Turks (Mandel 1989b). This disregards the meanings attached to various types of head wear by various generations of women in rural and urban Turkey. The deeply ironic predicament of the headscarf as a cultural marker and a symbol of an imputed 'Islamic repression of women' also has serious implications for ethnic hatred in Germany. A young neo-Nazi who had attacked foreigners and other socially vulnerable people such as homeless and disabled persons, confessed that he basically 'hate[d] these women with the headscarf' (*Die Zeit* 1.1.1993). Conversely, a German neighbour of the women and children who were murdered through arson in Solingen, believed that he had achieved good relations to his Turkish neighbours: 'these Turkish women were well integrated, they did not even have headscarves'.

Another Islamic prescription shows even more starkly how the negotiations of religious meanings in the diaspora proceed in a new field of post-migration dynamics. The Muslim ban on eating pork has led many Turks to adopt the definition of the dominant German discourse about who is a Muslim. The question of eating or not eating pork is irrelevant in Turkey, and the almost obsessive preoccupation with it is strictly a migrant problem. Similar to the headscarf having become a symbol of Muslim Turks in Germany, the ban on eating pork is one the best-known Islamic practices accessible to the German public. Although post-migration Turks have organized themselves to solve the problem of providing *halal* meat for the Muslim Turkish community, the solution is not free of conflicts and problems with German society as well as within the Turkish community. The general concern with the ritual cleanliness of meat and other food products is very widespread and is, I argue, partly reinforced through outsiders' definitions of what being a Muslim comprises. By the time they enter school, children are fully aware of the ban on eating pork, and Turkish parents usually avoid giving their children salami sandwiches to take to school, lest they be mistaken for pork. Ironically, non-pork salami is available in many Turkish shops.

Mosque organizations likewise demonstrate an excessive fascination with dietary detail (Ahmed 1992: 25-26). They distribute lists of common food products found in most supermarkets, which indicate items thought to contain pork, fat from pork, or alcohol. During my interviews with Turkish families, women especially expressed their frustration and anger; a mother complained how some of her guests, 'supposedly better Muslims', refused to eat the meat she had cooked. They asked her where she had bought it, implying that it might be mixed with pork or simply 'unclean' because of improper slaughtering methods. She vehemently defended herself, avowing that pork would never enter her house, that her family slaughtered their own animals,[14] and that she had prepared the very meal to celebrate her parents-in-law's return from the *hajj*. Along with the headscarf, the ban on pork and the elaborate precautions to avoid it have become visible markers to distinguish religious boundaries. They underline an emphasis on visual aspects of identifying a Muslim, as opposed to the invisible and implicit criteria of belief and ethics.

The influence of the non-Muslim environment, as well as the competition with it, are most clearly visible in the area of religious celebrations and Islamic organizations. Many parents express their helplessness and dismay at having literally to re-create the meanings and joys of celebrating

Islamic religious holidays for their children. The dominant Christian culture and the ways in which Christian celebrations address children exert pressure on Muslim parents, as well as on Islamic organizations, to make conscious, active, and positive efforts. Parents admit to the lack of atmosphere in their own religious celebrations, an atmosphere they believe existed in their childhood at home. To compensate for this loss, they make painstaking efforts to reaffirm the importance and meaning of religious holidays. Buying new clothes or shoes for their children, cooking meat and special sweets such as *baklava,* visiting older relatives (*büyükler*) and close friends are the minimum standards for almost all families. Explicit censure meets those Turkish neighbours who do not take a day off on Islamic holidays: 'even if one does not celebrate it as one did at home [in Turkey], one should not work like a slave and ignore the religious celebrations'. Islamic organizations go a step further and try to develop new forms of celebration, such as celebrating the *bayram* (*Hajj* or Ramadan celebrations) in the mosque, with food, presents, films and games for families or women and children together. More recently, weddings have begun to be celebrated in mosques. The social centre character of churches is taken as a model by mosques, and they offer services like conference programs, discussion groups or sewing courses for women, as well as sports activities for children and teenagers.

Concluding remarks

To describe the post-migration culture and religion of Muslim Turkish migrants in Germany requires attention to the issues of power and agency in minority-majority relations. Muslim Turkish and Christian German views of each others' religiosity and religion are indexical to various other debates concerned with modernity versus traditionalism, secularism versus fundamentalism, liberalism versus conservatism, integration versus ethnic isolation, racism versus multiculturalism – all of them debates which are particularist and global at the same time. Any analysis of the individual and collective commitments in post-migration culture and religion has to face the problem of distinguishing analytically between 'culture' and 'religion'. The discussion above has tried to show that this distinction is feasible at the level of exploring contact and interaction with another world religion. The migrants' notions of Islam and of its compatibility with Christianity show considerable flexibility so long as they can be accommodated within notions of cultural adaptation. German notions of their Christian religion, on the other hand, emphasize its cultural elements at the expense of all other possible effects from world religions such as Islam. German views of the changes within the Islam of Turkish migrants reflect a concern with maintaining religious boundaries, so that these changes are identified as cultural rather than specifically religious. The analytical and discoursive boundaries of religion and culture are rendered most visible in those instances where syncretism in culture is welcomed and accepted, but syncretism in religion is seen as undesirable or categorized as cultural. Examples of the former case may be seen in German notions of the 'cultural' integration of minorities; examples of the latter in Turkish, as contrasted to German, validations of religious syncretization. These mutual dynamics require all the more analytical attention as they refer not only to the debates on minority-majority relations and multiculturalist politics, but also to the very role of religion in 'postmodernity'.

Notes

1. A previous version of parts of this paper has appeared under the title 'Are Fireworks Islamic? Towards an understanding of Turkish Migrants and Islam in Germany' in *Syncretism/Anti-Syncretism: the politics of religious synthesis* (eds). C. Stewart and R. Shaw, Routledge, London, 1994. I would like to thank Gerd Baumann for comments on this version. The arguments in this paper are derived from a research project at the University of Bamberg, Chair of Islamic Studies, on 'Islamic socialization among Turkish migrant families'. The study has been carried out from 1990-93 in Nürnberg, where I have lived since 1988. It explores the types of Islam being mediated at home and in the larger context of the diaspora. Research methods include qualitative interviews with household members (8-9 year old children, 14-15 year old teenagers, and parents) from 30 Turkish migrant families, and with Turkish teachers and *imams*, as well as participant observation at schools and in mosques.

2. The interview was carried out at the beginning of January 1991, shortly after the Christmas holidays.

3. She became a devout Muslim after her migration to Germany. In her interview she associates the recovery of her honour through Islam (*islam'la şeref buldum*) with her perception of the Christian religiosity of various of her acquaintances. She is one of the explicitly 'devout Muslims' in Nürnberg, and in public wears a '*çarşaf*' in the street, a black shroud covering her whole head and body. She often takes part in local public discussions on women and Islam, is active in a Muslim womens' group in Nürnberg and acts as the correspondent abroad of a militant Islamic womens' journal (*Mektup*) published in Turkey.

4. This point can be related to Gerd Baumann's discussion of convergence and encompassment in this volume, although in the present case the two traditions converge only in so far as they are recognized as equivalent. The difference here may be due to the unequal power relations between the two traditions. The woman's position reflects the strategy of encompassment, as she constantly refers to Jesus Christ as 'our', i.e. the Muslims' Prophet, implying an all-encompassing quality of the Muslim Divinity. At another point during the interview, she underlined this quality by claiming Germany and all Europe as Allah's territory, so that Muslims had an intrinsic right to live here, albeit as loyal citizens of a God-fearing state. Correspondingly, her critique extends to the secular regime in Turkey as well.

5. I heard this story from school children, adults and Turkish Islamic religion teachers. It is told with a touch of disbelief, but nevertheless with the purpose of demonstrating the superstitious elements within Christian practice. The logical inconsistency, namely of Germans 'misunderstanding' a Turkish word, did not seem relevant to those I talked to. The story was not to be interpreted in terms of its logical consistency, but as a mythical text, where unusual things are expected to happen in any case.

6. By the term 'exotic flavour' I refer to the famous debates in anthropology on 'rationality'. I am weary of the questions which might be raised: do Turks really believe in such things? Similar 'exotic stuff', such as the idiosyncratic explanation of the connection between 'eating pork and the inability to be sexually jealous' among Germans have been discussed by Schiffauer (1988: 255). The point I try to raise here relates less to the 'exotic' content of these stories than to the complexity of the process of their production; a warning against any simplified analysis attempting to 'discover a Muslim cosmology' or 'mental structure' is appropriate here.

7. For a critical assessment of this type of restricted culture concept, see A. Çağlar (1990).

8. For a very similar usage of the term 'migrant Islam' see Saint-Blancat (1993), who actually uses 'migrant Islam' and '*Islam transplanté (en Europe)*' interchangeably.

9. E. Özcan's (1987) study shows that there are 3000 Turkish immigrant organizations (*Vereine*) in Germany, 1000 of them political, 600-800 athletic, 500

Islamic-religious, and 500-700 cultural and social. There are also ca. 28,000 Turkish members of the Social Democratic Party of Germany (*Die Zeit,* 11.6.1993); those who hold German citizenship have the right to be elected as party officials.

10. For an elaborate and distinctive discussion of state, society, the position of Islam in the Ottoman Empire, and the changing relations between them in modern Turkey, see Mardin (1989), especially Chapter III, pp. 103-146.

11. For an extremely critical view of these ideological studies on language, culture, and history, see Beşikçi (1977), who argues that the reasons for the reification of the 'pre-Islamic' lie in the suppression of the Kurdish national identity and movement, whereby the ideologists sought to propose a continuous and common culture for the peoples of Anatolia, and hence for both Turks and Kurds.

12. By 'German classes' here are meant the 'regular classes' (*Regelklassen*) peculiar to the Bavarian educational system, where the classes are composed of mostly German pupils with a minority of foreigner children, and the language of tuition is German. The alternative, which is largely optional, is the 'national class' (*Nationalklasse*), where children are all of one nationality and the language of tuition is primarily the language of that particular nationality. Turkish children attending 'national classes' are taught by native Turkish teachers. The implications of these two types of class for the socialization of children are highly significant, especially in terms of establishing early and lasting types of contact and friendship ties among children of varying nationalities.

13. See Göle (1991) for a political and historical discussion of the implications of female dress and their significance for the modernity project of Turkish democracy. See also Kandiyoti (1991).

14. Many Turkish families in Nürnberg slaughter their own animals, although this is not, strictly speaking, legal. Usually a few Turks come together and make an arrangement with a German farmer from a village in the vicinity and there slaughter the animal themselves. Alternatively, they hire a Turkish Muslim butcher to do it for them according to the religious prescriptions. Various mosque organizations carry out the task of slaughtering on a larger scale and follow the German regulations; they regularly sell this meat to their members.

References

Ahmed, A.S.
  1992   *Postmodernism and Islam: Predicament and Promise.* London: Routledge.
Beşikçi, I.
  1977   *Türk-Tarih Tezi, Güneş-Dil Teorisi ve Kürt Sorunu.* Ankara: Komal.

Binswanger, K. and F. Sipahioğlu
1988   *Türkisch-islamische Vereine als Faktor deutsch-türkischer Koexistenz.*
Benediktbeuern: Rieß-Druck Verlag.

Çağlar, A.
1990   Das Kultur-Konzept als Zwangsjacke in Studien zur Arbeitsmigration.
Zeitschrift für Türkeistudien 1: 93-105.

Die Zeit (1.1.1993) 'Den Haß krieg' ich nicht mehr los'.

Die Zeit (11.6.1993) 'Dossier: Drinnen vor der Tür'.

Elsas, C. (ed.)
1983   *Identität: Veränderungen kultureller Eigenarten im Zusammenleben von
Türken und Deutschen.* Hamburg: E.B. Rissen.

Göle, N.
1991   *Modern Mahrem: Medeniyet ve Örtünme.* Istanbul: Metis.

Kandiyoti, D.
1991   End of empire: Islam, nationalism and women in Turkey. In: D. Kandiyoti
(ed.), *Women, Islam and the State.* London: Macmillan.

Lutz, H.
1991   *Welten verbinden: Türkische Sozialarbeiterinnen in den Niederlanden und
der Bundesrepublik Deutschland.* Frankfurt/Main: Verl. für Interkulturelle
Kommunikation.

Mandel, R.
1989a Ethnicity and identity among migrant guestworkers in west Berlin. In:
N.L. Gonzalez and C.S. McCommon (eds.), *Conflict, Migration, and the
Expression of Ethnicity.* Boulder, London: Westview Press.
1989b Turkish headscarves and the "foreigner problem": constructing difference
through emblems of identity. *New German Critique* 46: 27-46.

Mardin,
1989   *Religion and Social Change in Modern Turkey.* Albany: State University of
New York Press.

Meeker, M.
1991   The new Muslim intellectuals in the Republic of Turkey. In: R. Tapper (ed.)
Islam in Modern Turkey: Religion, Politics and Literature in a Secular State.
London: I.B. Tauris, pp. 189-223.

Miller, D. (ed.)
Unwrapping Christmas. London: Routledge.

Saint-Blancat, C.
1993   Hypothèses sur l'évolution de l'"Islam transplanté" en Europe. *Social Com-
pass* 40, 2: 323-341.

Schiffauer, W.
    1988   Das Eigene und das Fremde: Bemerkungen zum Wandel von Fremd- und Selbstverständnis im Prozeß der Arbeitsmigration. In: I.M. Greverus, K. Köstlin and H. Schilling (eds.), *Kulturkontakt – Kulturkonflikt. Zur Erfahrung des Fremden.* Frankfurt/M: Syndikat, pp. 185-199.
    1991   *Die Migranten aus Subay: Türken in Deutschland: Eine Ethnographie.* Stuttgart: Klett-Cotta.

Sirman, N.
    1989   Feminism in Turkey: a short history. *New Perspectives on Turkey* 3, 1: 1-34.

Stewart, C.
    1994   Syncretism as a dimension of nationalist discourse in modern Greece. In: C. Stewart and R. Shaw (eds.), *Syncretism/Anti-Syncretism: The Politics of Religious Synthesis.* London: Routledge.

Stewart, C. and R. Shaw (eds.)
    1994   *Syncretism/Anti-Syncretism: The Politics of Religious Synthesis.* London: Routledge.

Thomä-Venske, H.
    1981   *Islam und Integration.* Hamburg: E.B. Rissen.
    1988   The religious life of Muslims in Berlin. In: T. Gerholm and Y.G. Lithman (eds.) *The new Islamic presence in Western Europe.* New York, London: Mansell, pp. 78-88.

Werbner, P.
    1990   *The Migration Process: Capital, Gifts and Offerings among British Pakistanis,* Oxford: Berg.

Wilpert, C.
    1988   Religion and ethnicity: Orientations, perceptions and strategies among Turkish Alevi and Sunni migrants in Berlin. In: T. Gerholm and Y.G. Lithman (eds.) *The New Islamic Presence in Western Europe.* London: Mansell, pp. 88-106.

Convergence and encompassment

Two dynamics of syncretization in a multi-ethnic part of London

Gerd Baumann

This chapter aims at making transparent two dynamics by which the inhabitants of a multi-ethnic suburb of London deal with, and in turn often effect, processes of syncretization. I have called these dynamics convergence and encompassment, respectively. To understand the former, the ethnography must first distance itself from any dichotomy between a religious and a secular sphere. Hence in introducing the dynamics of convergence, I speak of it as civic-cum-religious. To understand the latter dynamic, that of encompassment, it may best be seen as a cognitive response that, on the one hand, denies the pluralist tone of local constructions of convergence, yet on the other hand can be equally productive of syncretizations.

The data originate from fieldwork in a suburb of London, named Southall, which comprises some 60,000 people.[1] Some 40,000 of these are of South Asian origins. Roughly speaking, half of these are Punjabi-speaking Sikhs who have migrated directly from the Punjab or indirectly, as the 'Twice Migrants' described by Bhachu (1985), from the East African countries. A quarter of Southall's South Asians are Hindu, mostly from the Punjab; and the remaining quarter are Muslim, predominantly from the Pakistani part of Punjab. Southall is thus known, more or less accurately, as London's 'Little India' or 'Chota Punjab'. The remaining third of all Southallians are Christians; many are of English or Irish extraction, but there are sizeable numbers also of South Asian and Afro-Caribbean Christians. To segment a population on these criteria, must of course raise questions. Too numerous are the cross-cutting cleavages by which boundaries of religion intersect with boundaries of language, regional origin, nationality, and what Southallians call 'race'. Yet the commonest ordering of these cross-cutting cleavages is a notional division into five communities, three 'Asian' ones distinguished by their religions, and an Afro-Caribbean and a 'White' one postulated on the basis of 'race'. The view that Southall represents a mosaique of five bounded communities is associated with the equally common conviction that 'all the communities must get on with each other', especially as the town gained a, largely unwanted and misleading, publicity for 'The Southall Riots' of 1979 and 1981. These confrontations between neo-Nazis, police, and local youth have entered British folklore as serious break-downs of 'race relations' and multicultural coexistence. The tenets of multiculturalism are indeed one of the foci of convergence that characterize Southallians' public discourse and often their management of relations with 'others' also in private.

Convergence: civic-cum-religious

By convergence I refer to a process of culture change in which separate traditions, let us call them A and B, come to approximate a further tradition C, originally alien to both of them. Unlike the established approach to syncretic processes, convergence is thus untouched by any implication of dyadic or direct exchange. Traditions A and B converge upon C each for their different reasons and following their own agenda and paths. They thus remain separate from each other and need not engage in direct exchange; yet in the process of converging, independently of each other, upon the same model C, they do increase their observable similarities. Such processes of convergence do not, of course, happen in a power vacuum. Rather, they proceed in a climate in which certain practices or conceptions, namely those of C, are privileged as being generally desirable or exert an overriding hegemonic influence.

Such a hegemonic influence is visible, not only behind Southallians' oft-voiced view that their 'town' consists of five bounded communities, but also behind the normative expectations of how these communities should be treated to achieve social harmony. Essential to the prevailing version of multiculturalism are the demands that 'communities and their cultures' should enjoy equal treatment and recognition, public resources, and 'representation' in public institutions such as political and civic bodies, the media, and, importantly for this paper, schools. Given the local distinction of three 'Asian' communities based on religion, the 'representation' of 'community cultures' in schools is thus easily equated with a representation of their religious traditions. This can appear all the more plausible as Southallians, and not only South Asian ones, may see threats to their own multicultural coexistence in the reports of 'religious' confrontations such as the movement for an independent Khalistan, the Rushdie Affair and its ramifications, and a host of other putatively 'religious' tensions from the international level down to, for instance, local decisions about planning permission for a mosque in a neighbouring suburb. The 'religious' predication of multicultural ideas about representation and community provision is enforced further by the central role that temples and mosques play, not only for the representation and incorporation of the Sikh, Hindu, and Muslim communities alike, but also in everyday life. Far from functioning only as places of worship and representation, they act in parallel to English 'community centres' as providers of leisure pursuits, and of advice and help in a plethora of daily difficulties and everyday matters.

Such everyday matters themselves constitute a powerful dynamic of civic-cum-religious convergence. Southallians, of course, are subject to the same hegemonic influences as other people in Britain. They watch British television, read British newspapers,[2] and find their life chances imbedded in the British and local economy. As importantly for the data that follow, they live in a country and town where religious worship is assumed to take place on a Sunday, where English is the *lingua franca* and often becomes the first language of the young, and where children are schooled according to the British 'National Curriculum'. These hegemonic influences are essential in understanding the more localized processes of convergence that I can turn to now.[3] These processes range from a convergence on certain practices to convergences of conceptions. I distinguish the two for methodological reasons: a convergence of practices may be observed by the ethnographer regardless of whether or not informants recognize it as such. To evidence a convergence of conceptions, the ethnographer clearly requires local endorsement, that is, for example, a situation in which Southallians of different religions explicitly state that 'our religions agree on such-and-such positions or values'.

Some of the practices on which Southallians of different religions have come to converge I have described elsewhere (Baumann 1992): many Sikh and Hindu families have converged upon celebrations of Christmas. Beside the sending of Christmas cards, these often involve seasonal decorations in the home, Christmas parties at schools and offices, and the exchange, on Christmas Day, of wrapped presents among family and friends. Some of these practices are for the benefit especially of children, and one would hesitate to ascribe to them too explicit a religious significance. Suffice it to say that Hindu and Sikh celebrations of the Christian occasion present a tangible example of a convergence by two traditions upon practices originating with a third.

Christmas

A less conspicuous moment of convergence, but one which may indeed subtly alter established religious conceptions, is shared congregational worship on Sundays. Southall's four Sikh Gurdwaras and two Hindu Mandirs all attract large numbers of believers for acts of worship on Sunday, and one may hear complaints that individual worship on other days of the week is in decline. 'Back home you go to the temple when you feel like it,' a member of a Mandir committee once told me, 'only here, people think that Sunday is Temple Day, and the rest of the week is not.' Such convergences of practices, and perhaps even conceptions, are implied also in standardized English-language glosses which have become common-place. Religious festivals are most readily glossed in phrases such as: 'Diwali is our Christmas' by Hindu and Sikh Southallians, and 'Eid is our Easter' by their Muslim neighbours. Larson even heard a little Muslim girl wishing for 'Eid eggs'. (Larson 1989: 72). There is, I think, more of conceptual substance in this engaging pun than meets the eye: the English language clearly serves as a point of convergence as much as Christian templates of Sunday worship or Christmas celebrations do. It is absolutely common-place to hear young Sikhs speak of the Ten Gurus as 'our gods' or, on the Judaeo-Christian as well as Muslim template, 'our prophets'. An Imam, a Gyanni and a Pandit are likewise referred to as readily as 'our priest' or 'their priest'. What may be most interesting about such linguistic convergences is what they imply in more general and cognitive terms. They lend plausibility to the common-sense view that different religions are comparable to each other and, more than that, are transformations of the same basic structure. Given the meta-vocabulary that convergent translations create, each religion has its own peculiar Christmas or Easter, prophets and priests, and its own inventory of a limited set of rules and injunctions. On certain injunctions, of course, they agree: 'It doesn't matter', as a young Sikh explained, 'what religion you're from: it's wrong to kill, and it's wrong to steal things, and you must have some respect.'

With regard to other injunctions, religions can be seen to permutate the same few basic possibilities: 'You see, the Muslims aren't allowed to drink, but they can smoke, and we [the Sikhs] can't smoke, but we can drink. So it's the same thing, only different, innit?' Or: 'The Muslims don't eat pork, and the Sikhs don't eat beef, and the Hindus don't eat meat at all.' The picture of religious variety that emerges from these and many other comparisons easily offered by school children and teenagers is effortlessly pluralist: all religions converge upon one matrix of defining features and are thus not only comparable but homologous; and each defines its peculiarity by selecting one or another of a limited common stock of injunctions, be they on diet or fasting, days of devotion, marital or funerary procedures. If young Southallians were trained as anthropologists (and to some extent they do the job for each other), their first choice of paradigm might well be a morphological variety of structuralism. Religions, at any rate, are described without scruples as mere transformations of the same basic structure.

The question must then arise how far this homology might go. Does it stop at structural form, or is it stretched to relativize also the hallmark of much dogmatic religion, the claim to metasocial truths? Is there evidence of explicit beliefs that go beyond the convergence of practices and recognize that different religions converge upon the same shared truths? More than once I had wondered, after discussing this with Southallians, what they might make of Mozart's (1791, KV 619) classic Masonic line:

'Die Ihr des unermesslichen Weltalls Schopfer ehrt,
Jehova nennt Ihn oder Gott, nennt Fu Ihn oder Brahma ...'

['Ye who revere the Creator of the immeasurable Universe,
call Him Jehova or God, call Him Fu or call him Brahma ...']

Southall was not, of course, a town populated by 18th century Free
Masons or, for that matter, haunted by the spirit of Lord Herbert and
echoing with ideas of 'natural religion'. Religious distinctions, differences, and disapprobation are of the greatest impact on 'community
politics' as on the competition for civic resources, as I hope to show in
forthcoming work. Even in the absence of 'community' competition,
Southallians still have to balance three contending factors: the concern,
among many, for the continued 'purity' of their religious tradition; the
demand, enshrined in the civic doctrines of multiculturalism, that all
faiths should enjoy equal representation and mutual respect; and finally,
of course, the need to deal, practically or cognitively, with the convergences of practice or conceptions, not least among the young. Yet statements such as Mozart's appeared to be echoed in statements by
Southallians such as this young man, aged 18, from a Hindu family: it is
taken from an interview about multifaith worship at school assemblies,
a matter which I shall shortly discuss in more detail.

Q.: So that [i.e. multifaith worship] doesn't bother you?
Hursh: 'No; all religions say the same few things.'
Q.: Really? What do they say? Can you –
Hursh: 'They say: God exists. And he is the creator. And secondly, be good;
and then if you are good, you'll have it good, either while you're alive or
maybe later.'
Q.: But don't they mean different things when they say God is the Creator?
Hursh: 'Well yes, God has a different character in each. Like the Muslim God
is a very strict God and wants submission. The Christian God is a more kind
God and giving and ... and for the Hindus, God is not like a father or a person,
but an entity, like Brahma, you know, an entity.'
Q.: And the Sikh God?
Hursh: 'That's not really so clear, because apart from God they believe in their
Gurus, and sometimes they think that these are Gods. But that's quite wrong.'

Such a statement clearly needs contextualising, and the following case
summary will help to do this, as well as shed some light both on the
extent and the tone of Southallians' ideas of convergence.

Convergence and the question of truth: a case summary

As in probably all matters of religious orthodoxy and syncretization, the enculturation of children holds a special significance also among South-allians of different faiths. The issues of religious education were thrown into clearest relief by new British legislation which stipulated the introduction of a National Curriculum for all publicly financed schools. Part of this new law was the demand that Daily School Assemblies were to contain 'an act of worship [...] mainly Christian in nature '(Education Reform Act (1988): 7). Morning assemblies in English schools have been regulated by law from the beginnings of universal schooling. They usually comprised various organizational announcements, summons and admonitions, the singing of a school or religious hymn, and a short act of worship according to the teachings of the Church of England or, in denominational schools, the Roman Catholic Church or the Jewish faith. Parents of other faiths retained the right to withdraw their children from these assemblies. In Southall schools, the preponderance of students from Sikh, Hindu and Muslim backgrounds had long made an explicitly Christian act of worship inappropriate, and had given rise to a routine of doctrinally pluralist, so-called 'multi-faith' assemblies. 'Most days,' a student summarized the situation, 'they read us a parable from some religion. Like, very often it's a Buddhist parable, and sometimes a parable from the Bible, or on Guru Nanak's Birthday, it's a parable from the Guru Granth, or on Holi it's a parable from the Ramayana.' Any acts of prayer were read out in English, with the instruction to 'close your eyes and be silent as we pray'.

The, almost proverbially English, pragmatism of this solution could no longer be maintained in the face of the new legislation. Although schools with large 'minority intakes' could apply to opt out of the 'Christian' bias enshrined in the law, the Act of Parliament could not be ignored. The political furore of a new law apparently endorsing Christian hegemony rendered school assemblies a matter of 'ethnic' and 'community' politics.

The following case summary relies on data collected during a day conference sponsored and hosted by the local town council, which assembled local politicians, civil servants, school teachers, and the

representatives of local temples and mosques to deliberate upon their
response to the new law. The sponsors and hosts were members of the
Labour Party and not unhappy to find in the Education Reform Act a
stick to beat a 'racist' conservative government. Of the other participants,
few were aware of the actual daily practice as it had evolved over two
decades in local schools. Space does not allow me here to give a *verbatim* account of the day's proceedings. Instead I offer a diagram which
summarizes the choices for daily school assemblies that participants
came up with or implied in the course of their discussions.

Diagram: Southallians' models for school assemblies

	SINGLE-FAITH ASSEMBLIES		MULTI-FAITH ASSEMBLIES	INTERFAITH-ASSEMBLIES
	(1)	(2)	(3)	(4)
attendance:	separate	joint	joint	joint
worship:	separate	separate	separate	joint
	(5)			
attendance:	joint			
worship:	joint			

As the diagram shows, the thirty or so Southallians identified and supported four major models of school assemblies, be they for each faith
by itself or for all faiths together. Notably, one further option, namely
that school assemblies should be altogether secular, was denied any
local support. The suggestion, put forward by an education officer of
Afro-Caribbean background, was given short shrift by the assembled
Southallians. The civic discourse of secularism was effectively countered
by the discourse of multiculturalism, equally civic in origin: 'minorities'
and 'minority cultures', it was said, had to be 'represented' in schools.
That they were to be represented as religions, reflects not only the
context of the meeting, but also attests to the social salience of religions
delineations as outlined already.

The five options can be arranged, as they have been in the diagram,
in a sequence from the most particularist to the most pluralist. Option 1

foresees a separate assembly for the adherents of each religion, to be held every day or at least on some days. The argument was phrased with a strong reference to the bond between parents and children. 'Without separate assemblies, we will lose our children', and indeed, 'now that we can have separate assemblies, we will get our children back into the community.' The devotional education of the young, their purity of faith, and their continued commitment to a 'community' defined on the basis of religion represented the major rationales for this particularist option. A slightly less particularist option, here numbered 2, envisaged a rota of religiously specific assemblies which should be attended by children of all faiths. Active participation in prayer should be reserved for pupils of the 'host community' on that day, and some insisted that prayers should be spoken in the 'community languages', that is, Punjabi, Hindi, and Urdu or Arabic. Thus, purity of religious practice could be combined with a joint attendance which should ensure equal 'representation' for all, as well as an attitude of 'mutual respect'. This option enjoyed almost as much favour as the first, not least perhaps because it could make appeal to the civic values of multiculturalism and the 'representation' of all 'minorities' by means of a rota.

The third option envisaged a multi-faith assembly for all and thus more or less reflected the status quo in Southall schools. It differed from the status quo, however, in that it assumed the existence of active prayer, when in current practice all prayers were silent. Given the assumption of active worship by the youngsters themselves, any prayer in one religious tradition should be accompanied by a 'respectful silence' on the part of those brought up in another tradition. This option, strongly orientated toward the values of 'mutual respect', could be implemented every day, or else as an addition to the single-faith assemblies of options 1 or 2. It was regarded as a compromise with the usual drawback of failing to satisfy the advocates of either end of the spectrum.

A full and mutual participation by all children in the prayers of all others constituted the final two options envisaged by Southallians. One, in the diagram numbered 4, reflects what is known as the interfaith position, that is, a fully joint act of worship regardless of the traditions to which pupils or prayers belong. It was formulated in direct opposition to the particularist option 1. While this first option had been justified as a means to retain, or even regain, the youngest generation for their parents' religious 'community', the proponent of the interfaith option 4 insisted that 'we have already lost our children. Your kids are lost already! We have lost the precious time to put controls on our kids. If you want to keep your children, go back [to the subcontinent] ! Here, they are lost from the community. They are all in one big society now. All are together in English society. If we now introduce separate groups again, we are condemning our own [that is, the post-migration] society !' The result was, for the most part, stunned silence. Surprisingly, joint attendance as well as joint active worship reappeared in an option 5 which foresaw single-faith assemblies characterized by indiscriminate cross-participation. Though intended as a compromise, the option failed to draw much support.

Four points might be noted from this brief exposition. An obvious one is the sheer variety of options put forth by a mere thirty or so Southallians. It ranges from the most exclusive particularism to the most inclusive endorsement of partaking in the prayers of all other religions. Secondly, the data has shown the pivotal role that many parents assign to religion as a means of anchoring their children in 'their community'. Thirdly, a striking feature of the entire day's discussion was the unquestioned assumption that single-faith assemblies and even single-faith acts of worship were possible at all. The deliberations proceeded, not only as if all children were Sikh, Hindu, Muslim or Christian; but indeed as if there were no complication at all in delineating 'who' was 'what'. Nothing could have been further from the social facts. I have elsewhere outlined the ambiguities of the boundaries between Sikh and Hindu Southallians, and I need only mention here that Sikhs of lower castes may claim a Sikh identity and be denied it by other Sikhs; Sikhs may attend Mandir worship and still be identified as Sikh; followers of the Ahmadiyya Muslim faith are not regarded as Muslims by most other Muslim Southallians; and among Christians, of course, divisions range from the Roman Catholic to the Baptist, the Methodist to the Spiritualist. Yet throughout the discussions, religious identities were thought to be bounded clearly, unequivocally, and consensually. Finally, what seems to me striking is the entire absence, throughout the day, of any exclusivist truth claims. Even the proponents of particularist assemblies limited their argument to the civic discourse of multiculturalism in which each 'community' was to be 'represented' and none to be 'made to feel second-class'. Assuredly, the meeting was not a representative sample of Southallians. Yet it included men well-known for their confirmed religious convictions and personal forthrightness. Even these spoke in ④ a tone of value-free and pluralist multi-culturalism, as if everyone believed all religions to be equally legitimate and indeed equally true. Examining the data I collected in contexts other than public debate, it is most unlikely that many of the discussants believed this all the time. It is not uncommon, at least in private, to cast doubt on the legitimacy of a major religion or, more commonly, a minor subdivision or 'sect'. Furthermore, the organizers of the conference had, of course, followed their mailing list which favoured the members of elected temple committees, rather than the, often itinerant, Holy Men (*sant, guru, pir*) who, on their visits to Southall, re-inspire exclusivist paths to religious truths and contend for authority among those in search of authoritative statements.

Yet throughout the day, the only reference to religious truths came from a former member of a Sikh Gurdwara committee who, aged around 70, was by far the oldest participant. Contrary at least to my expectations, he declared himself in favour of both interfaith and fully cross-participatory assemblies. His rationale will move the discussion from convergence to encompassment: 'I am not more educated man. All I know is One God, One God, One God. *Sat sri akal*! – One God!'

At first sight, the emphatic statement may appear as the most condensed endorsement of religious convergence: the faiths and prayers of all religions converge upon the same ultimate Truth. Yet the truth of this very convergence is encapsulated in the Punjabi words 'sat sri akal', the central axiom of Sikh orthodoxy from Guru Nanak's writings on. Other religions and new practices such as interfaith worship are claimed, thus, to follow from the very truth on which Sikhism is predicated. The Sikh faith, in other words, is not one set of convictions that needs to be articulated with other sets, but a body of truths that encompasses all other approaches to God, be they true, false or indifferent. I see in this an inchoate example of the second dynamic that this paper is concerned with: an intellectual strategy which I have called encompassment. In using the word, I follow Dumont (1980: 239-245) but loosely. The tenets of multiculturalism as Southallians see and apply them do not allow for explicit hierarchization.[4] Nonetheless, the example just quoted implies that Sikhism encompasses, that is, contains within itself, all that may seem to run contrary to it, that is, all other religions. A further instance of such encompassment can now be seen to lie behind the strikingly articulate endorsement of religious convergence quoted previously. I resume the transcript where, first time round, I left off:

> [Hursh: 'That's not really so clear, because apart from God they believe in their Gurus, and sometimes they think that these are Gods. But that's quite wrong.']
> Q.: But doesn't this interfaith produce a mish-mash of religions?
> Hursh: 'I suppose it does. But I find that – quite sensible, really. I believe that Jesus is another reincarnation of Brahma, and Guru Nanak is, too. Only Mohammed is not, because he never said he was divine, and Gobind Singh and the other Gurus, – the same thing: Gurus are not Gods, and they never said they were.'

What appeared, at first sight, and was perhaps meant as, a whole-hearted endorsement of religious convergence, has turned, with a minimum of intellectual effort, into a claim of encompassment. Not only does the speaker adjudicate other people's comprehension of their own doctrines, but he explicitly encompasses the Messiah and even one Guru of 'Others' as reincarnations of Brahma, the divine 'entity' of his own faith.

The belief in convergence *with* the 'Other' and the claim to encompassment *of* the 'Other' are thus two faces of the same coin. What one dynamic grants, the other claims back. Thus is tolerance of, and more than that, civic equality with the 'Other' reconciled with an overarching, selectively encompassing 'own' claim to truth. Both of these dynamics, beliefs in convergence and claims to encompassment, can co-exist in the same social arena and indeed the same informants' minds. Under conditions which favour an observable convergence of practices, Southallians are able to postulate a convergence of conceptions among all religions and, at the same time, to claim that their own encompasses the truths of all others. Encompassment, however, does not undo the pluralism established by ideas of convergence. To encompass tenets of other faiths is in itself a process of syncretization. For who would doubt that a Hindu who sees Brahma reincarnated in Jesus has produced a classic instance of 'syncretism'? What matters, however, is not the collection of multicoloured 'syncretisms' perpetrated by one informant or another. Rather, it is to ask how syncretization proceeds, and I have suggested to see in convergence and encompassment two mutually reinforcing dynamics. If this dual dynamic pertains, it should be recognizable most clearly in the main arena of syncretization in Southall: the interfaith initiatives.

Convergence and encompassment : interfaith initiatives *dual dynamic of c and e*

The term 'interfaith' has, over the past decade or so, become a convenient short-hand label for a number of informal, as well as church-sponsored, groups and initiatives that aim at developing contact and interpenetration among otherwise distinct traditions of religious practice or faith. Such contact can range from 'dialogue' and the fostering of 'mutual respect' through the celebration of joint worship on the basis of 'mutual learning' and 'spiritual exchange' to fully integrated acts of worship that unite followers of different faiths.

In Southall, the Interfaith movement is an unusually well-resourced initiative which can draw upon the support of both the major Christian denominations. Thus the Anglican Bishop of Willesden has continued to foster various local groups devoted to interfaith dialogue under the programmatic title 'Christians Aware', and the Roman Catholic 'Westerminster Interfaith Programme' provides funding for a full-time organizer and an office in Southall. The partners in dialogue for these official initiatives are, notably, the smaller religious congregations, such as the Sikhs of Ramgarhia castes and mainly East African backgrounds; and the more marginalized such as the Sikhs of the *Nam Dhari* tradition who revere more than the Ten Gurus of orthodox Sikhism; the Ahmadiyya, followers of Ghulam Mirza Ahmad of Qadian whom other Muslims do not regard as fellow Muslims; the Ravidasi congregation of 'untouchable' castes (*chuhra, chamar*); and the few local Baha'i. I draw attention to this point, not to question motives, but to assess the representativeness of interfaith activities in Southall. They combine two rather unequal parties: on the one hand, the most established Christian churches, each with its tradition of colonial missionization and its perceived 'social responsibility' for the joint civil welfare of all in the post-immigration society; on the other hand, precisely those segments of religious opinion left out entirely from the local discussion about religious assemblies summarized above, and dependent upon alliances with those religious establishments seemingly furthest removed from them. Southall's *Nam Dhari*, for instance, must rely on an Anglican church, rather than a Sikh temple, to provide a space for their worship. The interfaith movement is thus supported most strongly by those congregations in Southall that, for reasons each of their own, recognize their interdependence most clearly and converge upon the same interfaith pursuits, originally external to each of them.

Joint activities range from lectures and seminars through an annual pilgrimage which visits churches, temples, synagogues and mosques throughout London, to intensive weekend retreats and shared acts of worship. The sharing of worship presents, of course, the gravest doctrinal difficulties. In practice, it therefore tends to rely upon those moments of convergence that are doctrinally least specific and can sustain the greatest polysemy. The three most important of these are sacred and bodily symbols, ritual forms, and issues of generalized concern.

The symbolism of lights, candles and lamps can thus stand, for instance, for the conviction that 'the lamps are many but the Light is One' (Westminster Interfaith Programme 1988: 3). The symbolism of the palm twigs of peace, likewise, can be made accessible to all, regardless of their doctrinal convictions. The same is true of bodily gestures such as the folding of hands, the crossing of arms or the act of carrying sacred things upon the head. Among the ritual forms which allow for a convergence of devotional experience, the most commonly used are silent meditation, commensality, and pilgrimage. Among the generalized contemporary issues on which the followers of distinct religious traditions can draw are 'the place of women in the divine plan', environmental issues that stress humans' 'stewardship of creation' regardless of creed, and the general public concerns such as inner-city deprivation, Third World poverty, and the evils of prejudice, Apartheid, and racism.

Even this short enumeration makes it clear that moments of convergence are essential to the functioning, and indeed the plausibility, of any interfaith initiative that wishes to steer clear of doctrinal challenge or conflict. As religious traditions claim their special status on the basis of divine revelation and metasocial truths, interfaith activities must rely upon those symbols, forms, and issues that are doctrinally non-specific and can build upon old, as well as foster new, points of convergence among people of different faiths. Yet to the guardians of doctrinal purity, this must already present the edge of a slippery slope. With the mediation of interfaith activities, all religions can be seen to converge on the same few symbols, ritual forms, and indeed moral judgements. These moral judgements, moreover, tend to differ in method, rather than outcome, from those of a conventional secular liberalism. There are, indeed, proponents of the interfaith movement who, in private at least, admit to their indifference toward the doctrinal 'niceties' and even criticize the 'ethnocentrism' of their official creed. Yet they are few and far between, and the question must arise how such powerful moments of convergence can be reconciled with the doctrinal and revelatory claims of any particularist tradition.

There appear to be three solutions to this conondrum that Southallians engage in to different degrees. The first is, to recognize the convergence of all or most religions upon a few basic truths which may be phrased almost as they were, above, by our Hindu informant. The genial simplicity of this young man's syncretizing ideas, however, is hard to imitate for adults brought up with a deep attachment to orthodox claims on truths divinely revealed. It sits particularly badly with people used to accept the doctrinal authority of synodal or papal pronouncements on metasocial truths. I shall return to this point. The second choice is the rather inconsistent belief in an all-encompassing Divinity which, however, revealed itself without transcending historical or geographic boundaries. This view may be implied when children and very young teenagers sometimes speak of 'the English God' as opposed to 'the God of Punjab' (Larson 1989: 93).

The third choice is to explain this convergence by drawing upon one's own tradition and staking a claim to encompassment. Thus, the leader of Southall's Ahmadiyya congregation explained that his 'movement believes that all religious leaders, whatever their faith, were chosen by God' whom one must presume to be Allah. Similarly, the Roman Catholic church has staked its claim to encompassment by drawing on St.

Augustine's syllogism that 'in a certain sense, Christianity already existed "at the beginning of the human race"' (Pontifical Council [etc] 1991: 25). The quote, doctrinally authoritative also for Roman Catholics in South-all's interfaith initiatives, is taken from a remarkable collaborative effort of the Pontifical Council for Interreligious Dialogue on the one hand and the Congregation for the Evangelization of Peoples on the other. 'Proclamation and dialogue are thus both viewed, each in its own place, as component elements and authentic forms of the one evangelizing mission of the Church. They are both oriented toward the communication of salvific truth.' (ibid.: 2) This Roman Catholic salvific truth can encompass the truths of all 'Others' since 'the inchoate reality of [God's] Kingdom can be found also *beyond* the confines of the Church, e.g. in the hearts of other followers of *other* religious traditions, *insofar* as they live evangelical values *and* are *open* to the action of *the* Spirit' (ibid.: 35, emph. added).

   The claim to encompassment as the counter-balance to a perceived convergence can indeed re-fuel the most exclusivist truth claims which, on the face of it, deny altogether any idea of religious pluralism: 'More than half of England's Anglican Bishops says that Christians are not obliged to believe that Jesus Christ was God, according to a survey published today. [...] It is indeed just reward for the tireless efforts and thorough positive and rational propagation of Muslim theologians [...] that we see today the endorsement of the Muslim viewpoint by prominent clergymen as regards the real status of Jesus Christ (on whom be peace)' (Bana 1988: 2). I quote this foreign pamphlet circulated in South-all not because Muslim theologians are any more 'guilty' of claims to encompassment than any other. All claims to orthodoxy must stoop to encompassment if they are to remain conclusive at all. Rather, the quote is chosen because it shows the interdependence of the two dynamics I have proposed in this paper. The more that some believers construct convergences between different religions, the more will others salvage the tenets of orthodoxy by drawing up strategies of encompassment to counter-balance the dissolution of exclusivist truth claims. Even such encompassments, however, can establish new, if perhaps unintended, processes of syncretization. In Europe, this joint dynamic has proceeded uninterrupted from the late 18th century; elsewhere it is older still. In some regards, there is thus nothing new about Southallians' belief in the convergence of religious truths or about their cognitive management of these convergences by strategies of encompassment. What is new, however, is the interaction of this joint dynamic with a discourse of civic, and seemingly secular, multiculturalism.

Notes

1. In addition to resident part-time fieldwork (1986-90), this comprised a period of fifteen months of full-time research made possible by a grant from the Leverhulme Trust, London. I am most grateful to its Chairman and Trustees, as to Professor Adam Kuper who, as my Head of Department at Brunel University, has been most generous in his organizational support and intellectual guidance. My thanks are further due to my new colleagues at the Research Centre Religion and Society, University of Amsterdam, in particular Peter van der Veer, Peter van Rooden and Patricia Spyer.

2. In addition, Punjabi Southallians in particular make extensive use of video, cable and satellite technologies to view Indian productions both for entertainment and religious devotion. See the work by Marie Gillespie (1989) whose support and friendship I have enjoyed throughout fieldwork and since.

3. The local dynamics were first worked out for a symposium on 'Syncretism and the Commerce of Symbols' hosted by the Institute of Advanced Studies in Social Anthropology, Gothenburg. I thank its Director, Professor Göran Aijmer, for his warm hospitality and his thought-provoking comments especially on the salience of hegemony for my argument.

4. This clarification I owe to Peter van der Veer who describes contrasting cases of Hindu/Muslim encompassment (van der Veer 1994).

References

Bana, Mohammed
    1984   *Jesus – as Only a Messenger.* (Pamphlet, 4 pp., circulated in Southall). Durban, S.A.: Islamic Propagation Centre International.

Baumann, Gerd
    1992   Ritual implicates "Others": rereading Durkheim in a plural society. In: Daniel de Coppet (ed.), *Understanding Rituals.* London and New York: Routledge, pp. 97-116.

Bhachu, Parminder
   1985   *Twice Migrants. East African Sikh Settlers in Britain.* London: Tavistock.

Dumont, Louis
   1980   *Homo Hierarchicus. The Caste System and its Implications.* Augmented
           translation. Chicago: Chicago University Press.

Education Reform Act (1988): London: Her Majesty's Stationery Office.

Gillespie, Marie
   1989   Technology and Tradition: Audio-Visual Culture among South Asian
           Families in West London. *Cultural Studies* III, 2: 226-40.

Larson, Heidi
   1989   Asian Children – British Childhood. Ph.D. Thesis, Dept. of Anthropology,
           The University of California, Berkeley.

Mozart, Wolfgang Amadeus
   1791   Die Ihr des Unermesslichen. Cantata for Tenor and Piano, KV 619.

Pontifical Council for Interreligious Dialogue and Congregation for the Evangelization of Peoples
   1991   *Dialogue and Proclamation. Reflections and Orientations on Interreligious
           Dialogue and the Proclamation of the Gospel of Jesus Christ.* Off-print of
           Bulletin No. 77 of the P.C.I.D. Vatican City.

Veer, Peter van der
   1994   Syncretism, Multiculturalism and the Discourse of Tolerance. In: Charles
           Stewart and Rosalind Shaw (eds.), *Syncretism/Anti-Syncretism: The Politics
           of Religious Synthesis.* London: Routledge.

Westminster Interfaith Programme
   1988   Newsletter June 1988. Southall, Middx.: privately printed.

Part III

Comparison: not ethnic cultures but collective contingencies

A historical approach to ethnic differences in social mobility
Creoles and Hindustanis in Surinam

Mies van Niekerk

Introduction

A recurrent theme of the social science literature on Surinam (the former Dutch Guyana) is the rapid mobility of the Hindustani community which, in just a few generations, has managed greatly to improve its social standing, and in doing so has closed the former gap between themselves and the Creoles. The Hindustanis (as East Indians are known in Surinam) are often considered a successful immigrant group. The image projected of Creoles, by contrast, is rather a negative one, and it is largely determined by some of the more visible male members of the lower class. It is a pertinent question, therefore, whether the image of both ethnic groups is predominantly determined by only one part of each group, namely the 'successful' among the Hindustanis and the 'unsuccessful' among the Creoles. To what extent can one speak here of an ethnic myth (Steinberg (1989), and how far can one discern collective advantages, perhaps related to 'cultural essences'? Are Hindustanis, for instance, 'more entrepreneurial' than Creoles? Or are such generalized ascriptions of 'character' and 'propensities' along 'ethnic' lines little more than explanatory short-cuts that obscure highly complex dynamics of history and collective contingencies? In order to answer these questions, I shall examine the development of the social position of both Creoles and Hindustanis in Surinam from a historical perspective.[1] How did the ethnic division of labour in Surinam come into existence, and what explanations can be found for the economic specializations of each ethnic group? Is differential social success linked to 'culture' in a reified sense, or are there other factors which could offer a better explanation? No less importantly, what role does the projected 'ethnic' image play in this process? To answer such questions implies touching on a number of sensitive issues. The explanation of differential social success of Creoles and Hindustanis would seem strongly influenced by certain taboos surrounding this subject. The sensitivity of the issue lies in the fact that explanations which point to cultural determinants are readily suspected of holding the ethnic group itself responsible for social success or failure. Cultural explanations are indeed often one-sided by not taking full account of the structural factors and power relations involved. On the other hand, structural explanations have tended to ignore the specific history and culture of ethnic groups. The problem thus calls for a two-pronged approach. I will begin by sketching the history of both ethnic groups and their relational social positions. This will show that the Surinamese economy did indeed favour an ethnic division of labour. In the second part, I will search for factors which could explain this division of labour. These factors relate, on the one hand, to historical circumstances and, on the other, to socio-cultural and economic criteria by which the groups in question can be distinguished.

Creoles and Hindustanis: a short history of collective social positions

My analysis will begin with a short description of the development of the social position of Creoles and Hindustanis in Surinamese society. My starting point will be the period in which the first Hindustani immigrants began to arrive in Surinam, that is, the period after the official prohibition of slavery in 1863.

Free and unfree labour
The greatest concern of the colonial government, as well as the planters, in the post-abolition period was the continued supply of labour to the established plantations. After a period of State Supervision (1863-1873), a period in which the government saw to it that ex-slaves would sign a labour contract, there were fears of a great exodus from the plantations.

These fears proved partly ungrounded. Naturally, many ex-slaves did flee the plantations if it was at all possible; yet their departures occurred more gradually than many had expected (van Lier 1971: 180-182; Kruijer 1968: 52). The abolition of slavery, however, coincided with a general recession which gripped the colony after 1863. A sharp decline in the demand for export sugar appears to have been its main determinant (van Lier 1971: 198-199). Sugar exports had reached their economic heyday long before Emancipation. A number of authors have theorized that the economic stagnation of 19th century Surinam could indeed be attributed to the late enactment of Emancipation legislation. A mode of production based upon slavery was no longer profitable with the onset of industrial capitalism, a situation already apparent in neighbouring British Guyana (Mulder 1960/61; cf. Heilbron 1982). Whatever the causes, the plantation economy of Surinam fell into deep crisis in this period.

To ensure an adequate supply of cheap labour for the plantations, the planters decided to import labourers. In 1870, an agreement was made with the British government which set in motion the importation of indentured labourers from British India.[2] By 1917, when the practice was stopped, over 34,000 British East Indians had made the voyage to Surinam (de Klerk 1953: 73). The arrival of these Asian indentured labourers forced down wages in the colony, just at a period when they were threatening to spiral. After all, the planters could no longer have control over the labour of the ex-slaves, and it was not hard for the ex-slaves to find elsewhere the minimal living they had become used to as plantation slaves (Kruijer 1968: 48). Thus, the immigration of labourers from Asia was designed, not only to ensure a supply of labour, but also to force down labour costs. While the ex-slaves had been the contract labourers of Surinam during then ten years of State Supervision, it was now the new Asian immigrants who were to take over this function.

Wage labourers and smallholders
Another method of ensuring a supply of plantation labour was an indirect method, namely to maintain control over land (Heilbron 1982). Ex-slaves newly released could not, of course, enter the market as free labourers. To be 'free' of plantation labour, ex-slaves would either have to sell their labour elsewhere, or else gain access to land in order to

sustain themselves independently. Surinam certainly had enough available land for the ex-slaves to settle and cultivate, thus reducing their need to work as plantation labourers. Heilbron (1982), however, has shown how control over land was used, by the planters, to ensure control over, nominally free, labour. In some cases, they took possession of fallow ground to avoid ex-slaves beginning to cultivate it. Nevertheless, the occupation of disused land offered the ex-slaves one method of establishing themselves as independent smallholders. They could also settle on privately owned estates or on so-called government settlements (van Lier 1971: 226-7). In both cases, they were able to cultivate a small plot of land whilst remaining available as plantation labourers during harvest time. Many were unable to sustain themselves and remained dependent on the plantations.[3] According to Heilbron (1982), all manner of intermediate forms, ranging from wage labourer to smallholder, sprang up as a consequence of the continuing dependence of small-scale agriculture on the plantation sector.

Although the relationship between small-scale and large-scale agriculture remained under strain for a long time, it was small-scale farming that was eventually to become the dominant sector. In the first instance, it was the emancipated Creoles who developed small-scale farming. Their most important crop was cacao, which they cultivated in areas bordering the great rivers of Surinam. Many of these farmers, particularly those who produced for export, came to enjoy a reasonable standard of living. Around 1900, however, many of these cacao farmers left the land and migrated to the town. Two factors were responsible for this drift to the urban area. Firstly, the cacao trees were plagued by a number of diseases which proved difficult to eradicate and secondly, good wages could be earned in gold mining and balata extraction. Although earnings in these new sectors were adequate, life remained wrought with uncertainty because of the temporary nature of the contracts offered to workers. What remains today of Creole small-scale farming can be seen in the district of Coronie where ex-slaves were able to buy up unprofitable plantations. Here, they worked the land, not as a communal domain, but instead divided it up into individual plots. The main produce of the Coronie farmers has always been coconuts although, since the 1920s, they have also been engaged in rice-growing. In two other districts, Para and Upper Surinam, ex-slaves also acquired their own plantations, but here the land was not divided. Instead, it was communally owned, and plots were allocated according to need. In addition to food crop production, timber industry formed the main activity. Farming was never highly profitable here, and many drifted to the town in search of work in gold and balata extraction. These districts have remained little changed until now (see van Lier 1971: 228-32).

Generally, Creole small-scale farming has been marked by various waves of migration to, and from, the town.[4] These movements can be mainly attributed to the economic structure of Surinam which, for a long time, remained a producer of raw materials without developing an industrial base (Kruijer 1968; Willemsen 1980). Employment opportunities fluctuated a great deal, and most of these fluctuations affected the Creole population. The geographic mobility of the Creole lower class has, to a large extent, been determined by this economic instability (Buschkens 1974).

In contrast to the Creoles, Hindustanis had to rely on agriculture for a far longer time. Since 1863 it had been government policy to stimulate the settlement of rural areas[5] and, in furtherance of this aim, the settlements mentioned above were created. Hindustanis who opted not to return to India after their indenture expired,[6] became tenant farmers on these government settlements.[7] They cultivated cacao, coffee and various other food crops. After 1895, the government pursued this settlements policy more actively to encourage small-scale farming. Until then, the main thrust of government policy had been to ensure a supply of labour for the plantations. The collapse of the plantation sector had, however, necessitated the development of small-scale agriculture. Besides, it was in the government's interest that Hindustanis remained tied to Surinam. It was decided, therefore, that they would not lose their right to return to their native country if they were to settle as smallholders on one of the government settlements. Surrender of this right was rewarded with one hundred guilders compensation. The other conditions of settlement on one of these government areas were to remain in force. Later, these favourable conditions were extended even further, and Hindustanis could, for example, also receive the premium of a hundred guilders if they settled outside of the government settlements (van Lier 1971: 235).

This latter option was mostly preferred by Hindustanis. So far as possible, Hindustanis settled outside the government settlements. This move was not, however, without its disadvantage. Within their own designated areas, the government attempted to create an infrastructure with adequate facilities such as drainage and roads. Outside of the government settlements, farmers were themselves responsible for the reclaiming of land, although they were compensated by the policy that, after two years, the land could become their property at no cost. This option was very attractive to Hindustanis coming, as they did, from severely overpopulated areas of the Indian subcontinent. They saw the non-government settlements as a route to gaining independent economic status (Speckmann 1965: 41). Particularly during the cacoa crisis of the early 1900s, many Hindustanis left the government settlements to establish themselves as independent smallholders. In many cases, they took over land from Creole cacoa farmers who had departed to town.

It was also during this period that rice production expanded enormously in Surinam. Although Hindustanis were not the first to introduce rice cultivation to the country (the Creoles had already been growing it for some time), they must be given the credit for the enormous expansion in production. Hindustanis began growing rice for their own subsistence, but soon branched out to supply the internal market. Later, rice became a major export crop, especially during the two World Wars. The rice booms encouraged even more Hindustanis to leave the government settlements and establish themselves as independent farmers. Hindustanis were thus responsible, not only for the massive expansion in cultivated land, but also for modernizing the cultivation of rice. The accumulation of capital that rice production allowed for came to form the basis for an improvement in the position of Hindustanis in Surinamese society at large.

Urban employment and education

While Hindustanis remained active in agriculture, at least until the end of the Second World War, Creoles engaged in a long process of occupational differentiation. With respect to social class differentiation, the Creole population had always been more markedly heterogeneous than the Hindustani. The word 'Creole' itself is, by definition, a collective term used to indicate a heterogeneous population in both economic and cultural terms.[8] For this reason alone, it is rather misleading to view the Creoles as a single group when contrasting them to the Hindustanis.

The occupational differentiation found among Creoles has its roots in the pre-Emancipation period. Already in the 19th century a broad middle class of free 'Mulattoes' and 'Negroes' had developed alongside an upper middle class dominated by Europeans in Paramaribo, the capital. Moreover, a large proportion of slaves was, already in this pre-Emancipation period, not employed in agricultural production. Van Lier points to the important fact that, by the middle of the 19th century, no less than 35 percent of the productive slaves were already employed as artisans or domestic servants (1971: 163). When slavery was thus finally abolished in 1863, many of their number were already in urban areas, while many more were soon to leave the land in search of urban employment. In the city, these groups came to form a lower middle class, or perhaps an urban proletariat (see van Lier 1971: 96-116).

While unemployment among the urban middle class had always been considerable, it was, according to van Lier (1971: 248), only after 1924 that this problem began to reach alarming proportions among the lower classes. This was due, among other factors, to a recession in the gold and balata industries. Although a revival in urban employment opportunities did occur during World War Two,[9] unemployment resumed to rise again after 1945. The growing informal sector found in Paramaribo is an indication of this massive unemployment (see van Gelder 1984). The collective economic situation of lower class Creoles has thus not been a continuously difficult one, but has instead been marked by a high degree of instability and insecurity (Buschkens 1974).

As mentioned earlier, unemployment has been a major problem among the urban middle class since the time of Emancipation. This was particularly true of urban-based artisans positioned, as they were, between the lower and the middle class (van Lier 1971: 249-50). The middle class even expanded in size, due to an increase in the numbers of educated Creoles. These more educated Creoles sought employment in both the education system and the growing civil service. More highly educated Creoles were to be found in the professions. Long after the end of the Second World War, Creoles still dominated the higher managerial functions of business and politics. Many Creoles have thus come to view education as their most important channel of upward mobility. The lead that Creoles could assume over the Hindustanis can, to some extent, be credited to their earlier participation in education, rendered compulsory in 1876. More significance, however, may be attributed to their strong orientation towards a Western lifestyle, including an appreciation of the need for education itself. From the early years of the 19th century, 'Mulattoes' had begun attending schools, and some continued their education in the metropolis, following the example of Dutch colonists who sent their children to the Netherlands to be educated (van Lier 1971: 111). Hindustani parents, on the contrary, were not initially interested in having their children educated and, in light of their putatively temporary residence in Surinam, the compulsion of school attendance was not strictly enforced by the colonial authorities (de Klerk 1953: 128-129).[10] This imbalance, however, did not persist.

From the turn of the century, and particularly during the 1920s, a degree of occupational differentiation could be observed also among Hindustanis. Their drift to the town was linked to the supply of food-stuffs to the urban population. In the vicinity of Paramaribo, agriculture flourished, and this development went hand in hand with an ever-increasing involvement of Hindustanis in trade, that is markets, shops, and transportation. Furthermore, Hindustanis began to engage in artisan occupations in the urban economy. In both spheres, they came into direct competition with the Creoles (van Lier 1971: 248; Speckman 1965: 230). The economic boom years of World War Two brought yet more Hindustanis to town. In these years, education also began to be a significant factor in the upward social mobility of Hindustanis. According to van Lier, the minimal participation of Hindustanis in secondary education may explain the limited size of the Hindustani middle class up to World War Two (1971: 221). The foothold they had managed to gain in both agriculture and trade would form, however, the basis for further occupational differentiation through education (see also Speckman 1962/3). Hindustanis are now to be found in almost all sectors of the economy. The strict ethnic division of labour that existed for so long has now largely disappeared, although there is still some measure of unequal distribution between the two ethnic groups in various spheres of economic activity.[11] The considerable economic advances of Hindustanis, and their drive towards securing their political interests, have caused ethnicity to become a factor of major importance in national politics (Choenni 1982; Dew 1978).

The ethnic division of labour: in search of an explanation

The developments in the social position of Creoles and Hindustanis described above make clear that the division of labour in Surinam is indeed ordered along ethnic lines, although this situation has drastically altered since the Second World War. How is this ethnic division of labour to be explained? Why, for example, did the Creoles turn their backs on the land? Did they develop, as is often thought, an aversion to agriculture and regard the farming of rice as 'typical coolie' work? What attracted the Hindustanis to farming, and how is their success in this area to be explained? Was it, as is often suggested, because they are industrious and thrifty? The emphasis of my analysis will focus on a threefold cluster of factors: the political and economic circumstances, socio-cultural characteristics of both ethnic groups, and the role played by both the formulation of the image of ethnic groups and ethnic ideologies. Any analysis of these factors must, of course, take account of Surinam's dependent position within the system of international power relations. Even without explicitly examining this factor, various aspects of this dependency relation will come up in my analysis. They are not, however, my primary concern. Here, I will concern myself with how, given the circumstances, the social position of both ethnic groups developed in post-slavery Surinam.

Economic development and government policy

There are a number of apparent reasons why the majority of Creoles left the land, whereas Hindustanis were drawn to agriculture. Some researchers have pointed to Creoles' supposed aversion to farming as an explanation for their meager participation in agriculture (cf. Speckman 1965: 46). Naturally, it is possible that ex-slaves did develop an aversion to the type of work they had been previously forced to endure as slaves.

Yet it would be an essentializing nonsense to involve this factor as characteristic of a whole group, which, moreover, needs no further explanation. Furthermore, there is sufficient evidence to suggest that, in fact, the opposite is also true. Consider, for instance, the fact that a number of Creole farmers became fairly prosperous during the period of State Supervision. Van Lier describes this achievement as the result of the personal initiative and exertion of the ex-slaves (1971: 229-230). Many ex-slaves did, of course, flee the countryside, a trend that began even before Emancipation in 1863. Yet in a very similar society, such as that of neighbouring British Guyana, many ex-slaves remained on the land (Lowenthal 1960: 793; Kruijer 1968: 163). In other words, a deeply-felt distaste for agricultural labour would seem to be too simplistic an explanation. What then can explain the drift of the majority of Creoles away from agriculture?

Four different factors have to be considered to find a plausible answer to this question. Firstly, one needs to consider the policy of both the planters and the colonial government on the question of the supply of labour to the plantations. As the planters were compelled to force down labour costs in order to sustain the profitability of an, internationally outdated, plantation system, they decided upon the importation of cheaper indentured labour. If the ex-slaves did not leave the plantations of their own 'free will' then they were forced out and replaced by Asian labourers. Some researchers have even suggested that the arrival of Hindustanis did, to a large extent, block any chance that Creoles might have had to attain a better economic position, particularly where agriculture was concerned (Choenni 1982: 51). A second consideration is the fact that ex-slaves had the opportunity to seek a livelihood elsewhere, both within and outside the agricultural sector, which would have freed them of dependence on the plantations. As we have already seen, many settled as independent smallholders, while others were lured by the higher wages offered by the gold and balata industries. The attraction of these two sectors was reinforced by the cacoa crisis which obliged many Creoles to seek a new livelihood. Thirdly, the conditions under which the Creoles had settled as independent farmers were wholly different from those of the later period in which the Hindustanis first began to set up as smallholders. The year 1895 is generally considered a turning point in Surinamese agrarian politics because it marked a change of policy from one of supporting plantation agriculture to one which encouraged small-scale farming. One consequence of this change was that the conditions of settlement for Hindustanis were more favourable than those for the Creoles. A fourth and final factor was the pulling power of urban employment opportunities and urban-based education. The attraction of the town did not, however, begin with Emancipation. Already before that time, anyone who had to live and work on rural plantations did so because of necessity only. It is, then, not surprising that Paramaribo continued to attract people from the countryside. Moreover, the town offered better employment and educational opportunities. In addition to economic necessity, the better living conditions in town also widely attracted Creoles (van Dusseldorp 1963: 40; Kruijer 1951).

A combination of all these factors would seem to go some way, at least, toward comparatively minor participation of Creoles in agriculture. But what explanation can be found for the Hindustanis' continued preoccupation with agriculture, and their high degree of success when compared to the Creoles?

One important factor was simply that, although the Hindustanis had been indentured of their own 'free will', once contracted they were no longer at liberty to leave the plantations. Unlike the Creoles, they had no alternative source of income but to labour in the fields. For a long time, indeed, they were forbidden to seek employment in gold mining and balata extraction. The only alternative economic activity open to them was food production for their own consumption or for sale on the market (Heilbron 1982: 214).

Hindustanis thus found their chance in agriculture and took it. As early as 1863, the government had introduced a modest rural settlement policy. From 1895, this policy was expanded and improved considerably, a decision of great advantage to Hindustanis. The more the government encouraged smallholding and thus tried to tie the Hindustanis to the country, the more advantageous the conditions of settlement became for this group (see van Lier 1971: 235; Speckman 1965: 38-42).[12] It was essentially this government policy which allowed Hindustani small farmers to settle under far more favourable conditions than the

Creole farmers had ever enjoyed. A third factor was the switch to rice production. This was made possible, in part, by excellent ecological conditions which were ideally suited to the creation of the necessary ecology for rice cultivation (cf. Heilbron 1982: 254). For reasons that will be detailed later, Hindustanis were in an ideal position to provide the necessary labour and expertise for rice production at an important historical juncture. A fourth and last factor were the favourable new outlets for food crops. Raising rice production levels was in line with the government's aim of import substitution and improvement in local food supplies. Particularly during the First World War, the production of rice increased enormously, as it did again during the Second World War. The smallholders who had settled in the Paramaribo region, producing the food supply for the town, were also to achieve a comparatively high standard of living. Here, they gradually gained control over the concomitant transport infrastructure and trade. The importance of these latter two factors can be ascertained by a comparison between the meager success of the Hindustani smallholders of Saramacca and the relative prosperity of the rice producers of Nickerie and Hindustani smallholders in the Paramaribo area. The Saramacca producers' limited success can be attributed, not only to inadequate land drainage, but also to their remoteness from the market (van Lier 1971: 236).

Family structure
Until now I have concentrated upon the historical circumstances which gave rise to the ethnic division of labour in Surinam, and I have said little of the characteristics of either ethnic groups. One element that is often mentioned as a contributing factor in the differential social success of Creoles and Hindustanis is the difference in their respective family structures. The success of Hindustanis is often deemed to be a consequence of this difference. In agriculture, as in trade or more generally entrepreneurship, the Hindustanis are thought to have an advantage over the Creoles (cf. Benedict 1979). The family structure of the Creole lower class, on the contrary, is often related to an unstable social position and to general poverty. It is not within the confines of this paper to solve this very complex question; nevertheless, I will examine some aspects of this subject here.

The patriarchal extended family system of Hindustanis would seem to have had various advantages for their position in Surinamese agriculture. The families of fathers and sons formed a good basis for both socio-economic organization and business management. Not only could labour be organized hierarchically around the authority figure of the father, but there was also no need for labour from outside the kinship network. This was one of the more significant factors which allowed family businesses to become competitive.[13] Despres (1967: 89) has shown how the availability of family members as a source of labour contributed towards an expansion in both scale and profitability whereby rice could be produced as a cash crop.[14] The Hindustani family structure was particularly advantageous as the interests of family and business coincided, thus enhancing the loyalty of individual members (Benedict 1979). The Hindustani family ideology dictates that family interests are placed above those of the individual (cf. Adhin 1960/61).

That the family functioned as one economic unit gave the Hindustanis an important lead in rice production because of the labour-intensive character of this agrarian activity. Particularly where land had to be reclaimed, and a system of drainage maintained, a fairly large labour force was needed. This was, in principle, a costly venture, and where capital was scarce, cheap family labour could function as a good investment (cf. Despres 1967: 92). Possibly, this partly explains why the Creoles did not switch to rice production after the cacoa crisis (cf. Heilbron 1982: 213). In Coronie, for example, still a Creole farming district today, the most important agricultural product was the coconut. During the First World War, however, attempts were made to grow rice, but bad organization and an inadequate water control created many difficulties for rice cultivation (van Renselaar 1963a: 476).

This latter factor also highlights two other aspects related to family structure, namely those of land ownership and inheritance rights. As Hindustani kinship structure was both patrilineal and patrilocal, matters of land inheritance were often more clearly arranged, and they entailed less fragmentation of property than was the case among Creoles. The bilateral family structure of Creoles gave every child an equal right to the land, whereas among Hindustanis only sons had rights of landed inheritance. In practice, however, inherited Creole land was often not divided. Thus, claims on the land use or the produce thereof could always be made by relatives living elsewhere. This, in turn, had a negative effect upon land and irrigation management (van Renselaar 1963a: 476; cf. Despres 1967: 48).

Agriculture for the Creoles remained largely at a subsistence level. If better wages were offered elsewhere, they left the land. These were mostly young men, leaving behind older people and denying the family an important source of labour (Heilbron 1982: 273; cf. van Renselaar 1963a: 477). Despres (1967: 88) showed that those who remained behind were quite able to maintain agrarian production, because this involved products, such as cacoa, which were not very labour-intensive. Although these were less profitable than rice, they did at least enable some family members to continue to produce for themselves or for the local market, whilst men could supplement the income with wage labour. Thus, Creole family structure was flexible enough to adjust to changing circumstances. The more diffuse character of the Creole kinship system did, however, entail some comparative disadvantages. Claims on land, or the profits thereof, by relatives living elsewhere remained a lasting drain upon the resources of those left behind. The same is true of income earned outside the agricultural sector. A man had to meet the many demands being made upon him: from his mother, children, wife, siblings and collateral kin. Van Renselaar (1963a: 478) even suggests that the mutual obligations of family members or fellow plantation residents had a strong levelling effect on the standard of living within the community.[15] On the other hand, this system of mutual rights and obligations could serve as an important social safety net during troubled times. The family system did, for example, facilitate the continuous migrations taking place between the land and the town, because a migrant could, in times of need, always fall back on his kin in either location (Despres 1967: 85; cf. de Bruijne 1976: 48-49).

Economic behaviour and ethnic image-forming
As I stated earlier, the contrasting histories of the Creole and Hindustani groups is frequently explained by reference to the distinctive character and presumed traits of each ethnic group. The literature on Surinam often mentions a second element, namely economic behaviour and

attitudes (see, e.g., Speckman 1963a, 1963b; van Renselaar 1963a, 1963b; cf. Sowell 1981). Put bluntly, the rise up the social ladder by the Hindustanis is said to be due to their ardour, sobriety and thrift. The Creoles, by contrast, are said to lack the right 'businesslike' approach to upward mobility. Their work ethic and preference for a consumption-orientated lifestyle are said to be obstacles to any possibility of social progress.

The question is, to what degree these presumed social traits of both ethnic groups are correct and, how capable they are of explaining the variant social positions of Creoles and Hidustanis in Surinamese society. It cannot be denied that their lifestyles differed in some respects. The extreme sobriety of the immigrants arriving in Surinam, and their ability to save something of even the most abysmal of wages was remarked upon from the very beginning (see, e.g., de Klerk 1953: 138). While Hindustanis arriving from India had long been accustomed to a low standard of living, the Creoles, by contrast, had for long taken example from the lifestyles of Europeans. Because of their social and geographic isolation, the Hindustanis had been able to retain their sober existence and could, therefore, remain unimpressed by Creole status symbols (Speckman 1963a: 463, 465). The earlier movement to urban areas by Creoles had only reinforced their aspirations to, and taste for, urban patterns of consumption. The later urbanization and social mobility of the Hindustanis, however, also influenced their lifestyles. Already in the 1960s Speckman observed a shift in both the perceived needs and patterns of expenditure of young urban Hindustanis. Their more consumption-orientated behaviour stood in marked contrast to the generation before them (1963a: 466). In other words, the contrasting lifestyles of the Creoles and Hindustanis can partly be explained by differences in lifestyle between the countryside and the town.

The renowned thriftiness of the Hindustanis can also partly be related to the family system discussed earlier. Collective budgetary control across several families is probably an efficient form of housekeeping. Yet their capital accumulation can be attributed more clearly to their increasing economic strength. The position of Hindustanis was generally more stable than that of lower class Creoles whose economic position had been characterized by periodic unemployment, geographic mobility and irregular income. These differences in economic stability and certainty probably help to explain the two groups' divergent economic patterns. As far as I am aware, this subject has been little researched. In his study of the economic patterns of both East Indians and Africans in British Guyana, Despres showed that African villagers did save less than their East Indian counterparts, but that African bauxite workers saved more than East Indian sugar workers. In the first case the Africans were poorer than the East Indians, while in the second the reverse was true: the East Indian sugar workers were poorer than African bauxite workers. In other words, the differences in saving patterns reflected the differences in economic position (1967: 94).

Despres (1967: 95) recognized certain differences in cultural values which might underlie the economic behaviour of each ethnic group. Creoles were thought more prone to spend their earnings on what they perceived as the most pleasurable aspects of life, while Hindustanis lived carefully and conserved their income for expenditures such as religiously-inspired rituals and festivals. Both would use their income consumptively, but the Creoles would tend to opt for immediate gratification whilst Hindustanis would commit their earnings to more long-term indulgences. Yet here again, a link can be made to the respective degrees of economic stability and certainty found within each ethnic group. A pattern of life punctuated by drastic fluctuations in income and expenditures was characteristic of at least a proportion of lower class Creole men (Brana Shute 1979; Pierce 1973). Women would, of necessity, be more future-orientated because they, unlike most lower class Creole men, had the prime responsibility for the care of children (cf. Buschkens 1974; Benedict 1979: 320-321).

Besides differing lifestyles and degrees of thriftiness, the two ethnic groups are also said to have different work ethics. It is thought that the social success of the Hindustanis, considered as a result of their intrinsic drive, was an achievement of their own making. 'The reputation of the group was in conformity with the facts: they were generally regarded as hard-working people', Speckman observed (1965: 52). Few would disagree that the Hindustanis were hard workers, although this reputation only came about when they had settled as independent cultivators on their own land (de Klerk 1953: 138).[16] Apparently, such industriousness is not then a characteristic of the Hindustani per se, but, rather, of the

Hindustani smallholder. It would seem that the difference of whether an individual is a wage labourer or an independent producer is all-important here.

Conversely, the Creoles were depicted as less industrious and less inclined to perform regular work. The Creole small farmer has, according to van Renselaar, always been a farmer with an 'agricultural worker mentality': always ready to quit the land if and when he could get a job that was more profitable (1963a: 479). Given the fact that Creole agriculture had largely remained at subsistence level, it is not surprising that so many left if they could earn more elsewhere. The comparatively high geographic and labour mobility among the Creoles could easily give the impression that they had little interest in working on a regular basis. It is, of course, possible that monotonous work came to be associated with slave labour, but this perception then has been reinforced in a later historical period when the economic structure of Surinam was completely unable to cope with such a large category of free labourers (cf. Kruijer 1968; Willemsen 1980). And when industrial development did take off, in the wood and bauxite industries for example, it appeared to be largely dependent on Creole labour.

Any attempt to interpret social success solely in terms of the economic attitudes and behaviour of ethnic groups would result in a decidedly one-sided explanation. Of course, these are important factors in explaining social mobility, but there are indications that the opposite may also be true: that economic attitudes and behaviour are a concomitant of socio-economic position. There seems then to be a complex relationship between behavioural characteristics on the one hand, and social position on the other. The perception of one's own social position, and the image others impose upon one's own ethnic group, play an important role here. I will consider this more thoroughly in the following section.

Ethnic ideology

While in the Hindustani case, explanations are most often sought to rationalize social success,the search with the Creoles is usually directed towards explaining social disadvantage. This cannot possibly be related to their actual social position, because on average neither of the two groups is any better off than the other. Probably the positive image of the Hindustanis is a consequence of their rapid ascent up the social ladder over such a short timespan. But this does not explain why so much emphasis should have been placed upon the Creoles' social disadvantage and the Hindustanis' success. Rather, the explanation points to the way in which an ethnic division of labour has arisen in Surinam, and to the manner in which this influenced the formation of ethnic images and stereotypes.

Of the greatest influence on the forming of the image of both population segments were the circumstances of migration and the differential treatment by the government and the planters. The feelings of enmity that the ex-slaves retained for the planters is understandable; already during the period of slavery they had developed a whole plethora of open and passive modes of resistance (Hira 1982). But that the planters came to view them as both unmanageable and untrustworthy after the period of State Supervision had less to do with their supposed character traits, than with some concrete circumstances: the higher wages the ex-slaves demanded (and could earn elsewhere), the low wages doled out to the contract labourers, and the planters' fear of disturbances that the presence of ex-slaves on the plantations could incite (cf. Heilbron 1982: 97; Kruijer 1968). For these reasons, many ex-slaves were forced off the plantations. On the other hand, some planters did employ a number of ex-slaves both as overseers and as labourers to do the heavier work. 'The Negro' was often thought to be more suited to this sort of physical labour than his Asian counterpart, and this perception is partly responsible, not only for the ethnic division of plantation labour but also for the antagonism between the two ethnic groups. This is not to say that Hindustanis were not resistant or even rebellious. On the contrary, various forms of resistance did occur, especially in the early period of their residence (see Hira 1982: 196-215). But the assumed temporary nature of their stay made their situation appear less intolerable than was the case among slaves. Hindustanis were, moreover, under the protection of the British administration in India, which was to protect the interests of East Indians living abroad. This, and the governmental supervision of planters' compliance with contracts, meant that the treatment of Hindustanis improved over time. At the risk of sounding complacent, the more they proved their worth in agriculture, the better they tended to be treated.

The greater antagonism felt by Creoles towards the planters in the post-slavery period is, then, related to the way they were forced to labour. The cultural mechanisms developed to resist their oppression resulted in patterns of behaviour that were interpreted in totally different ways by the planters and by the former slaves. What the ex-slaves viewed as a legitimate way to escape a slave-like existence was seen by the planters as evidence of the unreliable or untrustworthy character on the part of their workforce. The two interpretations were not of equal importance, however. I have mentioned earlier that the interests of the planters dominated politics for a long time. The national interest came to be viewed as identical to the continued existence and prosperity of the plantations. According to van Lier (1971: 239), the planters' vision dominated all others in Surinam until the 1920s. This included their ideas on the role of Creoles in the economic development of Surinam. The expected exodus from the plantations after the ending of State Super-vision was at first belied by the actual development. The later movement of the ex-slaves to town, however, seemed to confirm the image of 'the Negro' that had already developed among the planters. Although Afri-cans had originally been transported to Surinam on the presumption that they were admirably suited to agricultural labour, now they were per-ceived as unsuitable for agriculture, and they were supposed to have low standards of work ethic. Of course there was a labour problem, according to van Lier (1971: 239-244), because unemployment was ac-companied by a shortage of plantation labour. But the Creoles were simply no longer prepared to continue their slave-like existence, and this gave rise to the myth of the 'lazy Negro' (Kruijer 1968: 122). This myth could also be easily modified. Thus, the notion that 'the Negro' had little motivation to work was challenged by the evidence of the hard physical labour they performed in the interior of Surinam. Now, how-ever, it was said that they were, not so much lazy, as in need of varied work which suited their adventurous spirit (van Lier 1971: 243).

Turning against such racist images, van Lier states that the Creoles' behaviour can be completely explained by the social context in which they found themselves. 'The conduct of the Creole and the peculiarities which he shows as a labourer can be explained from clearly perceptible social and economic motives' (1971: 244). Not only can the image of the lower class Creole be disproved by facts, but it does not even do justice to the important contribution that this group has made to the Surinamese economy, as cacoa farmers, as labourers in the gold and balata industries, and later as workers in the bauxite industry. The negative image of the Creoles is, then, rooted in an earlier historical period when the 'labour problem' in the colony became associated with a particular section of the Creole population. The positive image of Hindustanis, on the contrary, is founded in the useful role they played after the period of State Supervision. This dominant ideology left its mark also in later historical periods. It would seem to have co-determined the image-forming that surrounded the differential success of Creoles and Hindustanis.

Conclusions

This chapter has addressed the question how the division of labour in Surinam came to be arranged along ethnic lines, and how this division between Creoles and Hindustanis is to be explained. Nowadays, of course, these ethnic groups can hardly be considered as two segments of one society with clearly distinguishable cultures. Rather, there seems to exist what Drummond (1980) has called a 'cultural continuum'. Moreover, ethnic identifications may refer to more than one category, which sometimes seem contradictory but which are not mutually exclusive. The identification as 'Creole' or 'Hindustani' is as authentic as the identification as 'Surinamese' (cf. Eriksen 1993).

Our interest here, however, was primarily the social success of both ethnic groups and the images and stereotypes surrounding it. A historical approach proved to be most valuable to avoid one-sided cultural, or culturalist, explanations. The differing social positions of the two ethnic groups appeared to be largely related to the introduction of the institutions of slavery and indentured labour, and the character of government policy regarding each of the ethnic groups. Undeniably, the Hindustanis reacted well to the opportunity structure that this new society presented.

The speed of upward mobility among some sections of this community is quite startling. Yet the notion that their social success can be completely accounted for by reference to some social or cultural legacy is far too one-sided an argument. Not only were they drawn to Surinam under a completely different set of circumstances than were the Creoles, but the political climate of the time was also extremely favourable to them. The interests of the colony were centered on their remaining after the termination of their indentureship, and the government developed a generous settlements policy in the hope of inducing them to stay on permanently. The success of the indentured labour scheme, and the agricultural colonization which followed, reinforced the positive image of Hindustanis that, in turn, worked to their advantage in promoting further social success.

The institution of slavery, which forced the Africans to toil on the plantations, was a completely different starting point. Binding the ex-slaves to the plantations was difficult at first but, at a later stage, proved to be neither desirable nor necessary. The alternating push and pull factors drawing and repelling the Creoles to and form agriculture are an indication of the unstable economic climate of post-Emancipation Surinam. Agrarian government policy in this early period was not as favourable as it would later become to Hindustanis, while Creoles were also drawn to other economic sectors. The social relations between the ex-slaves and the planters were too strained to allow for a normal working relationship. The negative image attributed to the lower class Creoles, as well as their development of an oppositional cultural style as a response to their low social status, both originated from this early historical period. In so far as cultural values and behavorial norms play a role in explaining the social position of Creoles, it must be viewed against this background.

When being a Hindustani becomes associated with social success and being a Creole with failure, then one is obviously confronted with an ethnic myth. To begin with, the term 'Creole' is far too broad a category to be analytically meaningful. As I mentioned earlier, 'Creole' is essentially a collective term. It would perhaps be more realistic to compare the Hindustanis with those Creoles who, in the period of East Indian immigration, shared a similar social position with the new immigrants.

Although it would not be easy clearly to define such a category of Creoles, an analysis of this type would show that mobility from the lower to the middle classes also took place within the Creole group. No doubt there will also be a category of Hindustanis who have made little or no social progress. Furthermore, little credence can be given to a cultural explanation that fails to appreciate the importance of the long experience of racism that Creoles have had to endure. Of all the factors mentioned, it would seem that it is this historical experience that has been most influential in the ideology of social success. A final objection to this approach is the suggestion that 'success' and 'failure' are in some way related to an inherent culture characteristic of either group. I have tried to demonstrate that this is a one-sided argument which requires the corrective of a historical analysis of social circumstances.

Notes

1. This paper is based upon a literature study in preparation for empirical research to be carried out among Surinamese resident in the Netherlands. This research project financed by the Dutch Organisation for Scientific Research (NWO).

2. In addition to East Indians, Javanese labourers from the former Dutch colony of Indonesia have, from 1891 onwards, also been attracted to Surinam. Earlier attempts to encourage immigration from China, Madeira and the West Indies had little lasting success.

3. De Klerk reported that in the early years the plots allotted on the settlements were purposely too small. This then forced the smallholders to work part of their time as labourers on the plantations (1953: 163).

4. Around 1908, the migration patterns of Creoles reversed with the number of Creole smallholders increasing. After 1922, the trend began again to decline only to be revived as a consequence of the crisis in the gold and balata industries in the 1930's. In response the Creoles began to become involved in rice production (van Lier 1971: 233).

5. Following an 1863 decree, European migrants, Asian migrants who had completed their period of indentureship and those freed slaves who were exempt from State Supervision were allotted arable land. If, after two years, they proved to be capable farmers the land could become their property at no cost. The decree also made plot holders eligible for small loans (van Lier 1971: 226).

6. The immigrants were offered a five year indentureship after which they could claim free passage back to India. Contracts could also be extended yearly for a maximum of 10 years. The contract was between the government and the indentured labourer, the former seeing to it that both labourer and planter meet their contractual commitments. The contracts were subject to a 'penal sanction' and any breaches could involve the labourer being fined or imprisoned.

7. They were to pay nothing for the first six years of working settlement lands, after that they paid a yearly rent. It was not, however, possible to own the land (de Klerk 1953: 163).

8. As throughout much of South America and the West Indies the name 'Creole' in Surinam originally referred to Europeans born in the colony. Gradually the term came to be applied to American-born Africans as well. A 'Creole' became then any American-born individual whose ancestors came from overseas. After the arrival of Asian immigrants, the name took on a special meaning in Surinam: it came to be applied to Negroes, and those of mixed African and European descent (van Lier 1971: 2).

9. The economic growth of the War years was due both to the increased import-ance of the bauxite industry and the stationing of American troops in Para-maribo.

10. Between 1890 and 1906 so-called 'Coolie schools' were established to encour-age Hindustani educational attendance. Lessons were conducted in their own language. When it became apparent that the Hindustanis were to remain in Surinam the government then began encouraging education in Dutch (de Klerk 1953: 129-130).

11. The census of 1964 showed that the Creoles were then primarily engaged in governmental functions. No less than 40 percent of the Creoles were govern-ment employees, while only 15 percent of the Hindustanis worked as such. Agriculture occupied 44 percent of the Hindustanis, but only 7 percent of the Creoles (Dew 1978: 15). There was very little difference in regard to other occupations, except in mining and the service sector, were Creoles formed a majority. The service sector was predominantly occupied by female Creoles, while Hindustani women were over-represented in agriculture (Lamur 1972: 162). The data from the more recent 1980 census do not take ethnic origin into account in describing the occupational structure of Surinam making compari-son between then and 1964 impossible.

12. Of importance in this context is the role of the British authorities in overseeing the running of the indentureship scheme and, if necessary, taking steps to protect the interests of British East Indians. In 1895, the Surinamese authorities modified their policy towards the Hindustanis partly under pressure from the British (see, e.g., de Klerk 1953: 162-163).

13. This seems to have been the case with, for example, the Hindustani small-holders who settled around Paramaribo. Around the turn of the century they were able to out-compete the Dutch farmers who had previously monopolized the supply of food to the capital (Speckman 1965: 43).

14. Although Despres' analysis concerns neighbouring British Guyana, I think it is amply applicable to the Surinamese situation of the same period.

15. Pierce (1973) observed the same situation among Creoles in Paramaribo's lower class neighbourhoods. To what degree this ambivalence of mutual family commitments was also to be found among Hindustanis has not been well documented, at least not in the context of Surinam. Adhin (1960/61: 23) has shown that whilst the extended Hindustani family was in many ways advantageous, it was, however, a drain upon the potential of more able individuals as well as forming an obstacle to individual initiative.

16. De Klerk (1953: 138) considered the actual number of days worked by Hindustani indentured labourers, an average of between 180 and 190 per year, to be rather low. He also noted wide variations in reputation between various shiploads and categories of arriving indentured labourers. While some ships gained a good work reputation, others would be labelled as 'lesiman jahaz' or 'ships of the lazy' (ibid. 138-139).

References

Ahdin, J.H.
   1960/   Over de 'joint family' der Hindostanen. *Nieuwe West Indische Gids* 40;
   1961   17-27.

Benedict, B.
   1979   Family firms and firm families: a comparison of Indian, Chinese, and Creole firms in Seychelles. In: S.M. Greenfield, A. Strickon & R.T. Aubrey (eds.), *Entrepeneurs in cultural context.* Albuquerque: University of New Mexico Press.

Brana Shute, G.
   1979   *On the corner. Male social life in a Paramaribo Creole Neighborhood.* Assen: van Gorcum.

Bruijne, G.A. de
   1976   *Paramaribo. Stadsgeografische studies van een ontwikkelingsland.* Bussum: Romen.

Buschkens, W.F.L.
   1974   *The family system of the Paramaribo Creoles.* 's-Gravenhage: Martinus Nijhoff.

Choenni, Ch.
1982   *Hindoestanen in de politiek. Een vergelijkende studie van hun positie in Trinidad, Guyana en Suriname.* Rotterdam: Futile.

Despres, L.A.
1967   *Cultural pluralism and nationalist politics in British Guiana.* Chicago: Rand McNally.
1970   Differential adaptations and micro-cultural evolution in Guyana. In: N.E. Whitten & J.F. Szwed (eds.), *Afro-American Antropology. Contemporary perspectives.* New York: The Free Press, pp. 263-287.

Dew, E.
1978   *The difficult flowering of Surinam. Ethnicity and politics in a plural society.* The Hague: Martinus Nijhoff.

Drummond, L.
1980   The cultural continuum. A theory of intersystems. *Man* 15: 352-374.

Dusseldorp, D. van
1963   Geografische mobiliteit en de ontwikkeling van Suriname. *Bijdragen tot de Taal-, Land- en Volkenkunde* dl. 119: 18-55.

Th. H. Eriksen
1993   Formal and informal nationalism. *Ethnic and Racial Studies* 16, 1: 1-25.

Gelder, P.J. van
1984   *Werken onder de boom. Dynamiek en informele sector in Groot-Paramaribo, Suriname.* Diss. Universiteit van Amsterdam.

Heilbron, W.
1982   *Kleine boeren in de schaduw van de plantage. De politieke ekonomie van de na-slavernijperiode in Suriname.* Diss. Erasmus Universiteit Rotterdam.

Hira, S.
1982   *Van Priary tot en met De Kom. De geschiedenis van het verzet in Suriname 1630-1940.*

Klerk, C.J.M. de
1953   *De immigratie der Hindostanen in Suriname.* Amsterdam: Urbi et orbi.

Kruijer, G.J.
1951   Urbanisme in Suriname. *Tijdschrift van het Koninklijk Nederlandsch Aardrijkskundig Genootschap* dl. LXVIII: 31-63.
1968   *Suriname en zijn buren. Landen in ontwikkeling.* Meppel: Boom.

Lamur, H.E.
1972   *The demographic evolution of Surinam 1920-1970.* The Hague: Martinus Nijhoff.

Lier, R.A.J. van
1971   *Frontier society. A social analysis of the history of Surinam.* The Hague: Martinus Nijhof [1949].

Lowenthal, D.
1960   The range and variation of Caribbean societies. In: V. Rubin (ed.), *Social and cultural pluralism in the Caribbean.* Annals of the New York Academy of Sciences 83: 786-795.

Mulder, G.C.A.
1960/6 Suriname's economische stilstand in de vorige eeuw. *Nieuwe West Indische Gids* 40: 73-76.

Pierce, B. E.
1973   Status competition and personal networks: informal social organisation among the nengre of Paramaribo. *Man* 8, 4: 580-591.

Renselaar, H.C. van
1963a   Het sociaal-economisch vermogen van de Creolen in Suriname. *Tijdschrift van het Koninklijk Nederlandsch Aardrijkskundig Genootschap* dl. LXXX: 474-481.
1963b   De houding van de Creoolse bevolkingsgroep in Suriname ten opzichte van de andere bevolkingsgroepen. *Bijdragen tot de Taal-, Land- en Volkenkunde* dl. 119: 93-105.

Speckmann, J.,D.
1962/   Enkele uitkomsten van een sociologisch onderzoek onder Hindostaanse
1963   leerlingen van de Mulo-school in Nieuw Nickerie. *Nieuwe West Indische Gids* 42: 208-11.
1963a   De positie van de Hindostaanse bevolkingsgroep in de sociale en ekonomische struktuur van Suriname. *Tijdschrift van het Koninklijk Nederlandsch Aardrijkskundig Genootschap* dl. LXXX: 459-466.
1963b   De Houding van de Hindostaanse bevolkingsgroep in Suriname ten opzichte van de Creolen. *Bijdragen tot de Taal-, Land- en Volkenkunde* dl. 119: 76-91.
1965   *Marriage and kinship among the Indians in Surinam.* Assen: van Gorcum.

Steinberg, S.
1989   *The ethnic myth. Race, ethnicity and class in America.* Boston: Bacon Press [1981]..

Sowell, Th.
1981   *Ethnic America. A History.* New York: Basic Books.

Willemsen, G.
1980   *Koloniale politiek en transformatie-processen in een plantage-economie. Suriname 1873-1940.* Dissertatie Erasmus Universiteit Rotterdam.

Ethnic myth or ethnic might?
On the divergence in educational attainment between Portuguese and Turkish youth in the Netherlands[1]

Flip Lindo

Introduction

The variation in educational performance and occupational ascent between different ethnic minority groups has given rise to a debate, especially in the United States, about the relative importance of *attitudes*
and *class and opportunity structure* in explaining differences in social
mobility patterns between ethnic groups (see, e.g., Sowell 1981; Steinberg 1989). Major participants in this debate have been so inclined to
stereotype each other's position as to loose sight of the subtleties of the
interrelation of these explanatory categories. For social scientists who
do not work in experimental situations – that is to say most of us – it is
almost impossible to establish empirically the extent to which behaviour is
culturally or situationally defined. More often than not, a way of behaving
is culturally transmitted as well as fitting with regard to external constraints
(Hannerz 1969: 184).

Until now, anthropologists in the Netherlands have hardly addressed
the question what brings about differences in success among minority
groups, and what role the cultural or ethnic dimension may play in this
process. De Vries suggests that in Dutch society it is almost taboo to in-
quire into the possibility that members of a minority group might also be
impeded in their emancipation by aspects of their very culture (1990: 1).
Dutch studies which tackle the problem of the causes of educational
arrears among minority groups are mostly based on surveys among pupils. Quite a number of these have been carried out lately; most of them
conclude that the overall socio-economic position of post-migration

families is the most important, sometimes conclusive factor in explaining the lagging school performance of children from these families (Kerkhoff 1989; Driessen 1990; van Langen and Jungbluth 1990; van 't Hof and Dronkers 1993). Others claim that what they call the 'ethnic factor' actually plays an important role in explaining achievement and underachievement in education (see, e.g., Fase 1994). Most of these studies, however, lack any theoretical consideration of the notions of 'structural constraints', 'ethnicity', 'culture', and their interrelations. This is reflected in the rather haphazard choice of indicator-variables which, when examined more carefully, often contain a 'cultural' as well as a 'structural' element.[2] At a recent symposium on this subject, the participants came to the conclusion that patterns of analysis, grown from thinking in such mutually exclusive concepts, had led to an impasse.[3]

In the Netherlands it is particularly Penninx who has developed a model to make sense of the enormous amount of data that Dutch research on minorities has produced up till the end of the 1980s. Penninx's efforts to forge a theoretical link among the empirical facts concerning social position, group formation and ethno-cultural definition are very welcome, considering the conceptual chaos of Dutch minority research. However, taking his theoretical work seriously must mean that it should be critically viewed in the light of new empirical data. In this chapter I will examine whether a part of his model, in particular a pair of complementary concepts and their theoretical underpinnings, provide new insights into the first results of my recently concluded fieldwork. About the research I will tell more below. First let me introduce the concepts.

In Penninx's model the interrelation of micro- and macro-level perspectives plays an important role. Analytically, he distinguishes two aspects in the process of attaining a social position in society. Seen from the perspective of the individual, there is *position acquisition*: 'In this approach the individual is viewed as a protagonist who constantly makes choices and takes decisions, alone or as part of a network of individuals or a (small) group' (Penninx et al. 1993: 108). The macro-level approach is called *position allocation*: attention is given to 'structural factors in society [which] delineate and limit the scope of action of individuals, and pave prestructured paths for individuals in society' (108). In Penninx's view, position acquisition is a process initiated by individuals, institutions or organizations within the ethnic group. Position allocation, by contrast, is imposed upon them from outside the ethnic group, by the receiving society. Penninx stresses the importance of regarding these concepts as complementary; they should be studied together and in relation to each other as they refer to different aspects of the same process (Penninx 1989: 87; Penninx et al. 1993: 109).

Portuguese and Turkish immigrants in the Netherlands

The material on which this contribution is mainly based comes from my fieldwork among children of Portuguese and Turkish labour migrants in the Netherlands. Statistics and survey data indicate a large difference between the two groups in terms of overall school performance. The young Portuguese are quite successful in education, while their Turkish peers on the whole do poorly at school. Usually in such comparisons, a divergence in school performance of the young is matched by one or more conspicuous differences in the social position or migration history of the families of orientation. This is especially stressed in analyses by American and British authors of successful – often Asian – post-migration groups in their countries, which they explicitly or implicitly compare with marginalized segments of the black or West Indian communities. These latter groups have altogether different socio-economic backgrounds and histories in the receiving country (Ogbu 1987; Steinberg 1989; Cross 1994). In the present case, however, it seems more appropriate to begin by mentioning the resemblances, since these are striking.

In the expanding economy of the 1960s, Dutch industry was in need of labour; this need could not be met by the Dutch labour market. Large sectors of Dutch industry decided to recruit workers abroad, especially in Mediterranean countries. The Dutch government supported their efforts by concluding enlistment treaties with the governments of these countries, among them Portugal (1963) and Turkey (1964). Portuguese and Turkish migrants started to come to Holland in the same period: the second half of the sixties. In this period, only males in the age range between 20 and 30 migrated. Portuguese and Turkish migrants used proportionally the same channels coming to Holland: up till the 1980s there was hardly a difference to be seen in the percentages of Portuguese and Turkish migrants who came to Holland with an employment contract or as a 'tourist', sometimes invited by a relative or friend already in the country (Lindo and Pennings 1992). Portuguese and Turkish migrants exhibited virtually no differences in their levels of education; in their country of origin the majority of both groups had left school after finishing elementary education.[4] There is another correspondence in the fact that neither Portuguese nor Turkish migrants came to Holland with the intention to stay and build their futures in this country. This idea of being here only temporarily, to earn in a relatively short period of time the means to make a better future back home, was not given up when they decided to call for their families to follow them. That their children would grow up and take root in Dutch society was a consequence of family reunification which was initially hardly thought through. Against all the odds, the image of the Mediterranean immigrant as an 'international commuter' held out long in Dutch society. This is partly because the migrants themselves saw no reason to argue against it.

Of course, there are also differences to be seen in the available survey data about the two populations. First of all, there is a difference in scale. The Turkish group in Holland is much larger than the Portuguese. While, in the 1970s, the immigration of Portuguese and other South European groups stopped and their communities hardly increased further in size, the Turkish group continued to grow exponentially. After the government closed the borders to foreign workers, the most important channels by which Turks kept arriving in Holland was family reunification and (at times illegal) chain migration. By that time the Portuguese in Holland were already reunited with their families.

A related difference thus lies in the fact that it generally took Turkish immigrants longer than the Portuguese to reunite with their families. Thus, Turkish youngsters had more often to break off their education in Turkey and to re-start their school career in Holland at a relatively late age and without command of the Dutch language. This must, of course, have a negative influence on their educational performance. Nevertheless, even those children of Turkish immigrants who have been born and raised in the Netherlands and started their school career without these complications continue to show significantly worse results than their Portuguese peers.

In the 1970s and 1980s, major shifts in the economy rendered many labour migrants jobless. Although initially first-cohort Turks and Portuguese occupied the same kind of jobs, the Turkish group was struck much more severely by the closing down of traditional industries than the Portuguese. I have discussed this development in more detail elsewhere (Lindo 1994). One of the reasons is certainly that, although the difference in seniority will have been small in most cases, the principle of 'last in, first out' will generally have harmed the Turkish more than the South European migrants. In my qualitative research I chose to work with families whose fathers were matched occupationally, not only regarding the general level of their occupational position, but even, as far as possible, that position itself: most of the Portuguese and Turkish fathers of my informants work as employees of a big Dutch transport company in unskilled catering, cleaning, or portering jobs. Nevertheless, the children of these families show the same diverging educational profiles as indicated in the survey data.

It is striking that the underachievement of Turkish youth in education is not explained by unemployment. Ogbu (1987) mentions the demoralizing effects that a negative perception of post-school opportunities may have on the school attainment of some minority groups. Where it concerns a working or jobless father as a role model, no such effect is observable among Turkish families in the Netherlands. On this point the findings of my research are in line with those of quantitative studies: survey data record that children in Turkish families that are dependent on welfare exhibit exactly the same educational profile as their Turkish peers whose fathers have a job. Further, from my qualitative research data I cannot possibly conclude that Turkish children are discouraged to do well in school by bleak prospects on the labour market. They are aware of discrimination against their group, but time and again expressed to me their awareness that education is the only way to avoid those sectors of the labour market where discrimination is most intense.

The varying effects of racism and discrimination on the social position of Portuguese and Turkish migrant families are difficult to assess. At the bottom of the labour market, where competition for scarce decent jobs by undereducated youth is particularly fierce, it is possible that Turkish youngsters suffer the effects of a negative stereotyped image more than their Portuguese peers. Here, however, we are dealing with education. Research on the effect of expectations and conduct of the teaching staff on the educational career of migrants' children (of whom the great majority are Moroccan or Turkish) is contradictory. Recent reports conclude that these children get higher transfer-recommendations into secondary education than their indigenous peers (see, e.g., Mulder and Tesser 1992). Fase (1994) concludes that racism in the school context does not account for variability in educational achievement between minority groups, either in the Netherlands or in any other West European country. At the same time, not all schools are of the same quality, and the supposed negative effects of a high concentration of minority pupils in schools is often commented upon. Although it is not possible to draw conclusions on the basis of survey material, my qualitative research indicates that Turkish children, more than Portuguese children, go to so-called 'black schools' (*zwarte scholen*), i.e. schools with a large percentage or a majority of migrant children.[5] Research on the extent to which these schools influence educational attainment is, however, not conclusive.[6] A recent study concludes that Turkish and Moroccan pupils do better in 'black' than in 'mixed' working-class schools (de Lange and Rupp 1992). Nevertheless, the most important point to make here is that in Holland parents and children are in principle free to choose the school of their liking. There are hardly any financial impediments; and the structural hurdles to less 'black' or even 'white' schools, such as the distance between these schools and the neighbourhoods that Portuguese and Turkish families live in, or the lack of local knowledge that these families initially have, are overcome better by Portuguese children. As will be argued later on, interferences with the choice of a school spring to a large part from group-specific interaction patterns within the family and the community.

Seen through a long-distance lens, there are thus many resemblances between the two groups in terms of the education and skills acquired by the head of the family in the country of origin, as well as initial migration history and the allocation of positions in the Dutch economy. It is unlikely, however, that the enormous gap in educational attainment between Portuguese and Turkish children can be explained by these factors, or by other allocation processes in the host society, be they racism or the school situation. If the difference cannot be explained by macro-level external constraints, we should, in Penninx's scheme, consider those aspects of social manoeuvering which he would call acquisition processes. But how can these different acquisition processes, these 'choices and decisions made by individuals, alone or as part of a network or a (small) group' (1993: 108) themselves be explained? In Penninx's conceptual scheme, allocation and acquisition are two complementary aspects of the same process; yet if external constraints have so many elements in common, the difference in acquisition must be, at least partly, triggered off by something else. If individual choices and decisions lead to a significant divergence in statistical profile between the groups, they can hardly be brought about accidentally by personal or family characteristics.

It therefore seems advisable to shift our attention to processes which are at least partly cultural in nature. On may think here of group-specific patterns of behaviour that are not only a reaction to the changed circumstances, but are transplanted from the old situation into the new and are further transmitted after migration, in interaction with changing circumstances. I shall here deal first with the way in which these behavioral patterns are transplanted and reproduced in the Dutch environment. A later comparative analysis of this process will show up the limitations of a model that analyses micro-level interaction from a voluntaristic perspective.

I have no argument, of course, with the idea that position acquisition is in the first place a matter of individuals, or, sometimes, a small group of individuals closely working together towards a common goal. It is indeed conceivable, at least in theory, that a whole community or ethnic group might aspire to the same causes. Methodologically, however, it must be preferable to use concepts and models which are not, implicitly or explicitly, based on such assumptions of collective homogeneity. I have given some attention to Penninx's theoretical considerations because they render explicit a way of thinking which, in a more implicit and fragmentary way, can also be detected in the work of British and American scholars on differences in the school success of various minority groups.

Parental ambivalence towards education

Several published studies in the field explain disparities in educational attainment by positing collective attitudes, be they positive or negative, that relate to social mobility in general or to the domain of education in particular. These attitudes are thought to be holistically ingrained in the culture of the group. The authors thus speak of 'folk theories of success', 'educational strategies' and 'cultural logic' (Ogbu 1987; Gibson and Bhachu 1988; Pieke 1989). In my own research I found it difficult to discern any such encompassing group attitudes. Among the relatively successful Portuguese I could not, at group level, distinguish a 'folk theory of success', reflected for instance in folk sayings that might stress the value of formal education, as found among Californian Sikhs (Gibson 1987). Nor could I detect any overt parental educational strategies (Bhachu 1985; Ogbu 1987). Neither overt nor covert pressure was exercised on children to achieve in school, such as it is reported in studies on social mobility patterns of Asian families (see, e.g., Pieke 1989). Of course, some Portuguese parents show more enthusiasm about the educational attainments of their children than others. When talking retrospectively with parents and children about their school career it is, however, difficult to establish an unequivocal causal link.

As indicated above, Turkish as well as Portuguese immigrants in the Netherlands were reluctant settlers, and they certainly did not come here with the educational opportunities of their children in mind. My impression is that the interest of Portuguese parents is often roused *after* one of their children turns out to do well in school. Then, it is particularly the mother who tends to take an interest in following the child's educational achievements. Mothers tended to show pride in the school success of their children in a generalized emotional way, while fathers would often take a more distanced view, evaluating the achievements of their children in purposive terms. This means that they often react positively to good results, but sometimes question the benefit of schooling when their child does badly, reflecting on the negative effects of long school careers. Since many parents realize that they have little knowledge of the Dutch educational system, they leave the decision-making at various junctures to their children to cope with.[7] Many children thus experience a considerable freedom of action which can have positive as well as negative effects. Children might want to pursue a more or less ambitious educational career; they might also want to take it easy, or might choose a school solely because some members of their peer group are enroled there. Parents feel that they lack both the education, and the language ability to help their children with their homework. Some of them keep an eye on the time spent on homework and try to create supportive external conditions. Many others are content now and then to remind their children in a superficial way. There is certainly no negative attitude towards education; a positive element which is often stressed is that Dutch education is cheap in comparison with education in Portugal. The ambivalence of the educational aspirations of Portuguese parents is reflected in statements which I recorded many times, and in which they name themselves as a negative example: 'My children must go to school, otherwise they end up doing the same filthy job as I do', or: 'I say to them: "Look at me! Do you want to clean toilets later on?" But they have to decide for themselves!' That 'children have to decide for themselves' is a rider that one hears often, and it may reflect parents' awareness of their lack of knowledge to help, but also point to a lack of specific aspirations for their children. Remarkably, corresponding statements are also regularly put forward by Turkish parents. Following verbalized conceptions, one cannot conclude that education in Holland is held in low esteem. When directly asked, Turkish youngsters, like their Portuguese peers, will underline their parents' good will, but also their limited competence, in matters of education. Given such similarities, what then causes this difference in school behaviour between the two groups?

Interfering patterns of behaviour

The difference, I suggest, is to be found in patterned behaviours which stem from fields other than education but proceed to interfere with children's school behaviour and educational chances. These patterns of interaction are located in social relations within the family, and between the family and the ethnic community at large. Having described the way in which many Portuguese mothers support their children's school performance, I found that this behaviour implied no cultural emphasis on an educational career for the children. The crux, instead, appears to lie in Portuguese mothers' position in the family and their function as a link to the non-Portuguese outside world. These factors give a Portuguese mother more room to act than is, generally speaking, often allowed to Turkish mothers in their families. Portuguese mothers often have more contacts with Dutch neighbours and colleagues who can, at an early stage, provide informal information about Dutch education. Such information enables them better to defend the interests of their children vis-à-vis their fathers, and to support more effectively the childrens' demands for all kinds of things which they value in order to integrate in the school situation: acceptable clothing, permission to participate in social events, money for school outings, books and even computers. The position of Turkish mothers tends to entail less effective influence, especially when it concerns matters outside the home. This may, among other things, be connected to the fact that they finished elementary school significantly less often than Portuguese mothers, and that their participation in paid labour is very low indeed compared to that of Portuguese mothers, which in its turn exceeds the national average.

We should not conclude from this that Portuguese and Turkish post-migration housholds represent opposites on the same scale, with Portuguese families representing certain 'middle class' values, emphasizing negotiation between family members and Turkish families representing some 'traditional' type, where authority is solely bestowed on the father. There are certainly important differences in terms of household structure, domestic cycle, and kinship, some of which I will address below. Nevertheless, both Portuguese and Turkish families belong to a broad category of households in which the relations between fathers and children are typified by respect and a certain distance, and the relations between mothers and children by affection and closeness.[8] In such circumstances, the role of the mother as mediator between children and fathers is especially pronounced. Yet in Turkish families in the Netherlands, the position of mothers has been seen to be less effective in certain fields. Since in most cases they do not do paid work, they have far fewer contacts outside the community and less command of the Dutch language. In this way, they have less information and fewer arguments to put forward when they present their children's case to their husbands. Further, their expected role in the family is marginal when it concerns decisions on questions outside the home. Turkish fathers often take ad-hoc decisions without consulting even their wives, forced by obligations they have towards kin and co-villagers, and these can interfere with the educational career of their children.

Given the patriarchal family relations that are characteristic for Portuguese as well as Turkish households, the distance between fathers and their children is greater in Turkish than it is in Portuguese families. The deference which children pay to their parents, especially their fathers, is also ritually more pronounced. Rules of behaviour seem in the first place to serve the inculcation of traditional family relations. These rules, for instance, implicitly underline that sons fall under the authority of the father, irrespective of the fact that they may themselves be married and have their own children. In Portuguese families, by contrast, rules and practices of bringing up children are directed more often to the future independence of sons and daughters in their own families of procreation. These differences are accentuated by the fact that in the Netherlands, the extended family still retains a central place in the Turkish domestic cycle.

Migration, family and community

In most cases, migration has not greatly altered the relations between spouses and the position of wives and mothers in the first cohort of Turkish families.[9] To account for these persisting patterns of interaction, it is useful to point to the differences in the migration pattern of Portuguese and Turkish families. Throughout the sustained growth of the Turkish migrant group, chain migration played an important role. This meant that Turkish families did not build their communities in Holland from scratch, but rather developed them on the basis of already established relationships (see, e.g., Engelbrektsson 1978; Böcker 1992). The result was a large number of tightly knit communities of co-villagers or of former inhabitants of clusters of neighbouring villages. These communities encourage not only strong local cohesion, but have used relations with kin and co-villagers to build up close ties with communities elsewhere in Holland and Western Europe, as well as, most importantly, with the villages and regions of origin (den Exter 1993). Membership of these communities is ascribed, and it can be very difficult, if not impossible, to withdraw from them.

The close relation between Turkish families and their surrounding communities reinforces traditional institutions and patterns of interaction within the family, and it militates against any accelerated change. The most effective mechanism by which these behavioural patterns are consolidated is social control. As in most local communities, social control is sanctioned by means of gossip, which can be of an extremely malicious nature (de Vries 1987). The structure of the social networks and the way in which these developed make social control extremely effective. Since the communities of origin are tightly incorporated in the local post-migration communities, the sanctions for breaking with dominant norms are severe: loss of reputation for a family can have devastating consequences, not only socially but also economically.

Unlike the Turkish population, Portuguese families in the Netherlands are not divided into mutually exclusive region- or village-based communities. Rather, the Portuguese population is concentrated in a few cities in the West of the Netherlands and maintains tightly knit communities. These, however, are too small in numbers and too diverse in origin to contain viable region- or village-based subsections. Their members came from many separate regions of Portugal, and chain migration played a relatively less important role. Families formerly unknown to each other started to organize themselves for various purposes, one of the most important of which was the establishment of Portuguese language courses for their children. In the beginning, local communities experienced various processes of fission and fusion due to political developments in the home country. Regional and village-based ties, however, never developed to a point at which they could dominate the community. This is why mechanisms of social control are far less well developed. Sanctions, such as a loss of reputation, do not normally entail a carry-over to the communities of origin.

Portuguese youngsters, too, complain about gossip and its effects, but comparing their stories with those of their Turkish peers makes it clear that there are important differences in character and severity. There is a certain malevolence in most kinds of gossip, of course, and the brand that Portuguese migrants, and especially women, engage in is not altogether harmless. Portuguese mothers are often active in the community, for instance in the Portuguese church, or in related institutions that care for the sick and the elderly. Apart from visiting each other at home, they meet when collecting their children from the Portuguese school, and of course at the numerous feasts and festivals held throughout the year. There is thus plenty of occasion to gossip. When the victim is a young male, he usually experiences it as merely annoying. Girls, however, are more vulnerable, and persistent gossip can seriously threaten a girl's position vis-à-vis her parents. Wives of the first migrant cohort tend to say that they have more freedom of action in Holland than in Portugal, and it is generally felt that migration has improved their position vis-à-vis their husbands. Social control in the communities of origin is thought to be more severe, and it is critically commented upon when they return from holidays (see, e.g., Brettell 1979).

Although Portuguese communities exhibit considerable social cohesion, gossip is a far less effective deterrent against deviant behaviour. When a family considers it cannot bear the suffering of public slander, it may indeed isolate itself from other Portuguese in Holland. Members will no longer visit the clubs and the Portuguese church, and stop attending the festivals. They may take to attending feasts in other Portuguese local communities in Holland, and keep contacts with one or two trusted families. Most importantly, their relations with kin and friends in Portugal do not usually suffer from such developments. In fact, I came across several families whose members had been active in the community in the past; over the years, their contacts with the community and other Portuguese had petered out for no special reason. Youngsters see the community as a structure of recreational facilities (sports and festivals) which one can frequent for a while with friends, and use to make other friends, preferably of the opposite sex. Annoyed by the gossip this evokes, they may then decide to 'stop coming for some time', which however does not mean that they stop seeing their Portuguese peers. They frequent other places with their friends among whom there may be Portuguese which they know 'from the community'. The Portuguese community is, in some ways, tightly knit; in others, it meshes into Dutch society relatively smoothly.

In comparison with Portuguese youth, the networks of Turkish young people appear far more restricted. The limited range of action for girls is well documented (see, e.g., de Vries 1987). Although Turkish boys enjoy more freedom than their sisters, it is striking that only few of them develop stable friendships or participate in peer groups that they themselves value in a positive way. Many parents tend to welcome their children's relations with people from their own regional network, and as these networks are often locally confined, young people frequently have difficulties in finding peers with whom they can develop friendships. When asked about the essence of friendship, Turkish youngsters, much more often than their Portuguese age mates, define it in terms of what it is *not*: people who misuse your generosity, who cheat on you, or worse, lead you astray, are not friends. In this way they echo their parents who never tire to alert their sons to be on their guard against peers, be they Turkish or Dutch, who might lead them astray. Many young people's 'best friend' is a cousin who may live in another town or even another country (Belgium, Germany or Turkey), and whom they see only at intervals. Among the peers on whom they rely for more regular or daily company, one will not seldom find kin or fellow-villagers who are in Holland only temporarily, often without legal status. These tend themselves to lack even basic contacts with native Dutch society and often do not speak the language. The lack of enduring, multi-stranded relationships with native Dutch society, and the lack of variation in contacts with schoolgoing peers bring about a certain paucity of examples and role models for effective school behaviour. Children from Turkish families who are not included in village-based local networks have markedly more stable relations with native Dutch and Turkish peers from their neighbourhood or school environment.

As the examples above have indicated, ethnicity, or the ways in which cultural difference is communicated, play a role of varying importance among the first cohort of both communities. In the Turkish case, it finds expression in parents' fears lest their children 'become Dutch', that is to say, take over habits of native Dutch peers which are considered unsuitable. Turkish boys may be allowed to have Dutch girlfriends, but this indulgence may have less to say about broad-mindedness than about the status of, and stance towards, unrelated women. Parents do not wish to be confronted with them, and in the vast majority of cases it is out of the question that such a relation could be permitted to become serious. Most girls are not even allowed by their parents to entertain close contacts with native Dutch girls; a Turkish girl spotted talking to a male Dutch fellow pupil may seriously damage the reputation of her family and risk severe sanctions. No less revealing in this context is the distrust with which Turkish youngsters of different regional origins approach each other. Marriage between youngsters of different region-based groups is still a rarity.

Parents' fears that their daughters and sons might, in adolescence, develop ties with undesirable peers of the opposite sex make them insist on the tradition of early marriage. Children use what room for negotiation they have, and sometimes successfully use the argument of education in postponing marriage for some time. However, those who come from families that participate in tight networks cannot resist the pressure for long. All in all, the prospect of entering into wedlock during adolescence has a negative influence on educational aspirations. In many instances, early marriage actually terminates school attendance. The regional dimension is concerned also in reviewing the negative instances. In almost all cases of cross-regional marriage among the parental generation, the degree of social control generated by tight region-based networks is recognizably lower. In these cases, parents are also less insistent on seeing their children marry so young. Within the Portuguese communities, marriages between partners of different regions of origin are entirely unexceptional, and there is no emphasis on early marriage at all. Many Portuguese parents do find it very difficult to accept a native Dutch partner for their son or daughter. Nevertheless, in the end a Dutch son- or daughter-in-law is often accepted since parents expect the new nuclear family to gain independence and attempt to forestall any subsequent cooling of relations.

These functions of boundary maintenance do, of course, have a cultural momentum of their own. In this instance, one must stress differences in kinship practices, and in the way in which the sexual reputation of future spouses is emphasized in the process of constituting new families. I have further related these differences to the structure of the post-migration community and the concomitant mechanisms of social control. Patterns of group formation showed clear differences in the ways in which families are incorporated into the local community and the ways in which post-migration communities are related to the communities of origin. These factors have led to differentiations in the maintenance of ethnic boundaries. So although the 'cultural stuff' that ethnic markers consist of pertains to old values which are central also to the communities of origin, the extent to which they are used in organizing group members vis-à-vis the surrounding society depends very much on recent historical processes and the formation of local communities.

Among the influences on educational attainment, it may be worth here to recall several factors. I have connected the position of the mother in the Portuguese and Turkish family, the relative effectiveness of her role as a mediator between her husband and children, and the effect that this may have on school behaviour. Further, I have commented upon the varying possibilities for children to develop stable networks which can merge into native Dutch society, thus extending their educational horizon. Finally, I have stressed the wide-ranging effects of marriage practices within and between groups. There are, of course, other connections that could be stressed when trying to elucidate the diverging educational achievements of Portuguese and Turkish youth. Among the group-specific patterns of expectation and behaviour which influence educational performance one may think, for instance, of the varying ways in which new conjugal bonds are integrated in the larger kinship system, and of the strongly diverging normative importance of reciprocity. These factors, too, however, need to be related to the differing ways in which the local communities of Turkish and Portuguese migrants came into being and continue to function.

Conclusion

Taken together, the factors discussed in this chapter constitute the beginning of an explanation for the divergence in educational attainment between Portuguese and Turkish youth in the Netherlands. These factors have a cultural history of their own, and they show an observable impact on the behaviour of migrants' children in Dutch schools. They might even be related to each other in certain structured ways. There is no evidence, however, for any coordinating principle by which these behavioural patterns might combine to determine group-specific attitudes or strategies towards education.

My discussion has laid stress not so much on the long-term genesis of cultural particularities, as on their impact due to relatively recent historical forces. Like ethnicity, these behavioural patterns should be seen to exist as a set of relations within a specifiable historical context, rather than as some primordial 'given' (Comaroff and Comaroff 1992: 66). More specifically, the influence that these patterns of behaviour exert on educational attainment must depend on the sanctions which can be implemented to uphold the relevant norms. The implementation of sanctions must, in its turn, depend upon the extent to which the post-migration family is bounded by the local post-migration community. This is directly related to the way in which the community came into being: the degree to which migration proceeded as chain migration determined the degree to which the migrant community was subdivided into mutually exclusive region-based communities, as well as the intensity of links with the respective communities of origin.

In focusing on Portuguese and Turkish youth in the Netherlands, I wanted to challenge the tendency to use concepts of structure, such as 'allocation processes', only when thinking of factors affecting social mobility from outside the post-migration community, while reserving concepts of culture, such as 'folk theories of success', when thinking of influences within that group. Attention to the historical development of these communities alerts us to two observations: that post-migration communities generate their own structures of constraint and opportunity; and that group-specific behavioural patterns are not only consolidated by cultural transmission, but also by sanctions and social control.

I thus argue against Penninx's model, which reserves allocation processes to macro-level analysis, and conceives of behavioral patterns at the group level in terms of 'personal characteristics, efforts and choices' only (Penninx 1989: 87). This would make it impossible either to account for diversity within the group, or to analyze the changes that come about at the group level itself in the context of relations of dominance and subordination. From the perspective of different categories of actors within the group, group-specific behavioural patterns are often apprehended with ambivalence, or experienced as impediments. Young people, to name but one example, have to take these impediments into account when they try to formulate and realize their social goals; yet they need not necessarily adhere to the underlying norms.

Notes

1. Thanks to Hans Vermeulen and Robert Warmenhoven for their comments on an earlier draft.

2. A good example is the SES-variable (socio-economic status) which is used in most of this research. Besides the level of occupation of one or both parents it contains their level of education. This last characteristic is at least partly 'cultural' in nature in that it is to a large part ideational in content (especially where it concerns its transmissive function on a cognitive and normative level in the family) and is almost always acquired in the country of origin, not allocated in the Dutch setting.

3. See for instance the contribution to this symposium of Latuheru and Hessels (1994).

4. During the period that the fathers went to school, elementary education in Portugal lasted four years, in Turkey five years.

5. I should add, however, that Portuguese children go there quite often too.

6. In the United Kingdom, too, research into the effects of the school has not led to agreement among scholars; see, for instance, a survey of research by Drew and Gray (1991), and Smith and Tomlinson (1989) followed by a debate (Gillborn and Drew 1992; 1993; Hammersley and Gomm 1993).

7. Until 1993 the Dutch school system compelled parents, teachers and children to make important choices immediately after finishing elementary school. Even at this early juncture many Portuguese parents do not take any initiative. Of course the educational staff tries to involve parents in these moments of decision,

and then Portuguese mothers do play a role: when children have different ideas about their educational career than the teaching staff, mothers tend to side with their children. I may here anticipate a difference that concerns Turkish families: Turkish mothers are less involved with the school of their children, and neither they nor their husbands are inclined to argue with staff advice about secondary education.

8. Sectors of the native Dutch working class also belong to this family type; there is, however, a strong decrease in the percentage of indigenous families which fall into this general category of 'command households' as they are called in Dutch sociology of the family (du Bois-Reynmond 1992).

9. One more reason why Turkish mothers are unable effectively to support their children vis-à-vis their husbands is that their children act in the Dutch environment which is often approached with distrust. Below I will touch upon this distrust as a theme in the organization of cultural difference. One could say that, after migration, the position of Turkish mothers as an intermediary in the family has got weaker, while that of Portuguese mothers, in their own view, has improved (see below).

References

Bhachu, P. K.
  1985   *Parental Educational Strategies: The Case of Punjabi Sikhs in Britain*. Research Paper in Ethnic Relations nr. 3., University of Warwick.
Böcker, A.
  1992   Gevestigde migranten als bruggehoofden en grenswachters: kettingmigratie over juridisch gesloten grenzen. *Migrantenstudies* 8, 4: 61-78.
Bois-Reynmond, M. du
  1992   Pluraliseringstendenzen en onderhandelingsculturen in het gezin. Bijdrage aan Sociaalwetenschappelijke studiedagen, Amsterdam.
Brettell, C.
  1978   *Hope and Nostalgia*. Ann Arbor: University Microfilms.
Comaroff, J. and J. Comaroff
  1992   *Ethnography and the Historical Imagination*. Boulder: Westview Press.
Cross, M.
  1994   *Ethnic Pluralism and Racial Inequality*. Utrecht: ISOR.
Drew, D. and J. Gray
  1991   The black-white gap in examination results: a statistical critique of a decade's research. *New Community* 17, 2: 159-172.

Driessen, G.W.J.M.
   1990   *De onderwijspositie van allochtone leerlingen.* Nijmegen: ITS.

Engelbrektsson, U.-B.
   1978   *The Force of Tradition.* Gothenburg: Acta Universitatis Gothoburgensis

Exter, J. den
   1993   Regionale herkomst van Turken in Nederland. *Migrantenstudies* 9, 3: 18-34.

Fase, W.
   1994   *Ethnic Divisions in Western European Education.* New York: Waxmann.

Gibson, M.A.
   1987   The School Performance of Immigrant Minorities: A Comparative View. *Anthropology and Education Quarterly* 18, 4: 262-275.

Gibson, M.A. and P.K. Bhachu
   1988   Ethnicity and School Performance: A Comparative Study of South Asian Pupils in Britain and America. *Ethnic and Racial Studies* 11, 3: 239-262.

Gillborn, D. and D. Drew
   1992   'Race', class and school effects. *New Community* 18, 4: 551-565.
   1993   The politics of research: some observations on 'methodological purity'. *New Community* 19, 2: 354-360.

Hammersley, M and R. Gomm
   1993   A response to Gillborn and Drew on 'race', class and school effects. *New Community* 19, 2: 348-353.

Hannerz, U.
   1969   *Soulside.* New York: Columbia University Press.

Hof, L. van 't, and J. Dronkers
   1992   Onderwijsachterstanden van allochtonen: klasse, gezin of etnische cultuur? *Migrantenstudies* 9, 1: 2-25.

Kerkhoff, A.
   1989   De geschiedenis herhaalt zich: onderwijskansen van allochtone kinderen. *Migrantenstudies* 5, 2: 32-47.

Lange, R. de, and J.C.C. Rupp
   1992   Ethnic Background, Social Class or Status? Developments in School Attainment of the Children of Immigrants in the Netherlands. *Ethnic and Racial Studies* 15, 2: 284-303.

Langen, A. van, and P. Jungbluth
   1990   *Onderwijskansen van migranten.* Amsterdam: Swets en Zeitlinger.

Latuheru, E.J. and M.G.P. Hessels
   1994   Onderwijsprestaties en de invloed van etnische en sociaal-economische herkomst: een statistisch dilemma. To be published in *Mens en Maatschappij.*

Lindo, F.
1994   Het stille succes. De sociale stijging van Zuideuropese arbeidsmigranten in Nederland. In: H. Vermeulen and R. Penninx (eds.), *Het democratisch ongeduld*. Amsterdam: Het Spinhuis.

Lindo, F. and T. Pennings
1992   *Jeugd met toekomst*. Amsterdam: Het Spinhuis.

Mulder, L., and P.T.M. Tesser
1992   *De schoolkeuzen van allochtone leerlingen*. Nijmegen: ITS.

Ogbu, J.
1987   Variability in Minority School Performance: a Problem in Search of an Explanation. *Anthropology and Education Quarterly* 18: 312-334.

Penninx, R.
1989   Ethnic groups in the Netherlands: emancipation or minority group formation? *Ethnic and Racial Studies* 12, 1: 85-99.

Penninx, R., J. Schoorl and C. van Praag
1993   *The Impact of International Migration on Receiving Countries: The Case of the Netherlands*. Lisse: Swets en Zeitlinger.

Pieke, F.N.
1989   Chinezen in het Nederlandse onderwijs. *Migrantenstudies* 5, 2: 2-17.

Smith, D.J. and S. Tomlinson
1989   *The School Effect*. London: Policy Studies Institute.

Sowell, Th.
1981   *Ethnic America*. New York: Basic Books.

Steinberg, S.
1989   *The Ethnic Myth*. Boston: Beacon Press.

Vries, M. de
1987   *Ogen in je rug*. Alphen a/d Rijn: Samsom.
1990   *Roddel nader beschouwd*. Leiden: COMT.

Greek-African interrelations in Eritrea and Greece
Social interaction as a framework for understanding the construction of ethnic identities

Marina Petronoti

Origins of the ethnographic question

The expansion of religious controversies, demographic upheavals and political persecutions, as well as the restrictions that northern Europe places on the entry of foreign manpower, have transformed Greece from a country of emigration to one which receives migrants and refugees from all over the world. Among these, there are large flows of Eritreans who seek asylum in Greece, together, notably, with Greeks who were born in but 'returned' from Eritrea. That these emphatically stress what they consider as vital differences between themselves and their compatriots, inspired me to investigate the process of identity construction.

Insistence on cultural or other variations is, of course, to be expected among those who are exposed to danger and delineate their stereotypical qualities in order to assess their social esteem. It is much less expected, however, among people who represent the majority tradition in their own country. This approach to ethnic identity is in line with the attention anthropologists pay to the link between ethnic identity and migration (Cole 1977; Tonkin, McDonald and Chapman 1989), but it differs from ethnographic works which focus on ethnic processes among minority groups.

Conceptualizing identity
I shall approach ethnic identity as a cultural construct in terms of which actors give meaning to their own and other people's belonging to a

certain group.[1] Such a construct not only depicts social representations and national history, but also reflects the perspective through which hegemonic principles and realities of the past are evaluated and reinvented in concrete social and historical settings (Hobsbawn and Ranger 1983; McDonald 1986). Indeed, anthropologists often underline the dyadic situations and contexts of opposition and relativity in which identity is created: self/other, familiarity/strangeness, past/present, etc. (Epstein 1978; Chapman et al. 1989: 18).[2] These challenging situations entail distinct kinds of behaviour: on the one hand, individuals preserve, partly at least, the institutionalized components of their cultural heritage, while on the other, they negotiate rigorously its symbolic meanings.

In conceptualizing ethnic identity as a cultural construct, I do not neglect its political dimension. On the contrary, I argue that ethnic processes are dynamic and multifaced (Barth 1969) and may in fact be seen as one aspect of social relationships in which cultural variations are communicated (Eriksen 1991: 27). The politics of identity construction denotes that every version of the 'other' is associated with self-perceptions and is expressed in schemes of social conventions, discursive practices, rules of preference and avoidance. Consequently, the ability to manipulate and reinterpret notions of identity raises questions about how people get involved with each other, aim to adopt prevailing types of behaviour, and make use of their cultural referents on varying occasions.

Such a conceptualization of ethnic identity is in agreement with Cohen's focus on the interdependence of this concept with access to scarce material resources (1974). I would suggest however, that in spite of its validity, this view should be slightly modified: the varied strategies that people utilize in their struggle for moulding perceptions of themselves and others manifest that the definition of 'us' and 'them' extends beyond the desire to accumulate wealth. Identity construction is political in a broad sense and should be seen as an inscription of interactive and communicative processes: when they consider it necessary, actors debate the nature of their identity in ways which cannot be reduced to economic interest per se, but relate to the increase of both their economic and their symbolic power through the acknowledgment of real or imaginary qualities by 'significant others'. The identification processes involved are thus in constant flux since actors experience and evaluate their stereotypical qualities in multiple ways which are historically and situationally defined.

In order to document these points, I utilize a social interactionist perspective (Goffman 1958; Berreman 1972) concentrating on people's interrelationships. I thus stress the choices they make among alternative kinds of behaviour in terms of the meanings which specific attributes, actions and situations have for them and for those with whom they interact; the criteria with which they classify themselves and others in various social and ethnic groups; and how these classifications affect their lifestyle, whether they change in time or in other people's presence.

As I will try to show, social interaction is a key indicator of ethnic identity. It is in fact possible to say that inasmuch as people who share the same values, cultural markers, language etc. interact more freely than others, one's identity may be discovered 'by the company he keeps' (Berreman 1972: 575). Effectively, investigation of social behaviour and relationships helps us to comprehend how ethnic concepts are defined and inter-ethnic ties work. Ethnographically, the questions I pose concern the ways in which Greeks from Asmara construct their identity with respect to Italians, Eritreans, and their compatriots in Athens towards whom they define their self-perceptions and manipulate their social image. More particularly, I examine the principles which underlie the development of their friendships over time, the ideals which underlie the characteristics they attribute to other ethnic groups, and the means with which they assert their cultural qualities. I shall enquire how essential it is for them to be regarded as 'Greek', what they do or avoid to do in the name of Greekness, what beliefs they draw upon to legitimize their views about cultural and social distinctions, and how far they set boundaries in contact with social inferiors. The analysis is based on life stories (Petronoti 1992) collected among Eritrean and Ethiopian refugees and migrants in Athens.[3] The material derives from Eritreans (who comprise one of the most active refugee groups in Greece)[4] and the second generation of Greeks who were born in Asmara – almost 90 people, the majority of whom settled in Athens in the 1970s.

Greeks in Asmara

Greeks arrived in Eritrea at the end of the 19th century: by 1902, 323 of them lived in Asmara and 146 in smaller towns (Papamichail 1950: 165-167). Their presence on the east African coast was due to job opportunities offered by Italians who had colonized Eritrea (1885-1941) and patronized industry, commerce, and public services. Although Greeks originally worked as manual labourers in the construction of roads and buildings, they soon played a key role in the local economy. They set up family enterprises, established commission and insurance agencies, grocery and ship chandler enterprises, trading companies, factories (of mineral water, sesame oil or cigarettes) and, on one occasion, a banana plantation (Papamichail 1950: 166-176).

'Where colour unites, access to political power divides'
Given the system of colonial rule, the first migrants were confronted with highly asymmetrical relationships and perceived themselves as an intermediary group between the colonists and the colonized. Their original intention was to take sides with neither of these groups. Yet, the development of their economic activities presupposed adherence to rules set by the Italian government: as many subjects recall, their parents had to keep a low profile, be obliging and pleasant, and avoid any hint of dissatisfaction with authoritarian structures. Such reverence was not of course, unanimous but varied according to the context of social interaction. Hence, Greeks were especially cautious in public arenas, but felt much less constrained when they were among friends: on these occasions they repeatedly stressed that they had 'nothing to do with Italians who ignore and violate human rights'. Accordingly, many refused to collaborate with them at work, did not participate in their public feasts, and even forbade their children to make friends at the Italian school: abstention from social relationships seemed vital since it was supposed to affirm the value they assigned to those of 'their own kind'. Behaviour towards the colonists was also defined by age and gender: young migrants were less conformist than the older ones, and men took greater offence than women at what they saw as the colonists' arrogant manners.

The resentment of the first generation of migrants was enhanced by Italians' negative posture. Colonists looked down upon pioneer Greeks who were poor and equipped with few or no skills and capital: judging from qualities which related to job situations, they regarded them as 'canny, insistent, with a propensity to bargain'. In return, Greeks strove to earn their living by 'honourable means', that is, means which would not endanger their social respect or cause disapproval. Autonomy at work was seen as an imperative: not only because a salaried job would augment their feeling of subjugation, but also because they associated it with an inability to prove their personal worth. Their social distance to Italian colonists was exacerbated by the Italian invasion of Greece (1940). This war was linked up with an admiring devotion to 'the glorious past of the Greek nation' and the revolution against Ottoman rule. These were sentiments which Greeks kept as a most precious 'memory' (Just 1989: 84): their ancestors' heroic example was to guide their practices and invigorate a desire for the continuation of 'national glory' in this small African country.

Preserving the cultural past: the foundation of the Greek community
The need to preserve their cultural heritage as a means of differentiating themselves among other ethnic groups, was probably the most important of the factors accounting for the foundation of a local community which had its own church (Evagelismos), a primary school (which grew to have 30 pupils in the 1970s) (Triantafyllou 1972: 38) and a club (which admitted Greeks and those who exhibited an amicable spirit).

In spite of the variations in their economic and occupational status (some, for instance, worked as employees to those who owned large firms) Greeks did not usually make distinctions based on wealth: rather, they reaffirmed their willingness to be together and have someone to trust and call upon in times of crisis. These ideals were clearly reflected in daily behaviour and relationships within the boundaries of their community: Greeks disseminated information about jobs and circulated books or small items connected to their common origin; they celebrated family rituals and national festivities wearing folklore costumes and preparing the required meals; gathered on religious ceremonies and exchanged gifts and food; preserved few ties with people of an alien religion; and were eager to display their Orthodox faith and knowledge of classic civilization. Women had a key position in these processes: they transmitted substantive symbolic carriers of identity (language, customs etc.) to the younger generation, thus producing subjects with clearly defined ethnic ideals and roles.

These elements bring to mind Cohen's point that ethnic groups whose interests are incompatible with hegemonic principles tend to articulate their internal organization on informal lines, making use of kinship ties, ritual and other symbolic activities (Cohen 1985: 108). In this sense, the foundation of the Greek community functioned as a social entity, the boundaries of which were symbolically as well as geographically marked and were primarily evaluated in terms of its members' interaction. The multiplex bonds they kept with one another manifested a desire to confirm their loyalty and belongingness to the same culture, while at the same time they exhibited their harmonious relationships to 'outsiders' who were not invited to their gatherings. For many years, relations outside their community remained impersonal and fragmented in contrast with the personal, holistic bonds sustained with 'those of their own kind'.

The dilemma of continuity and change
The ties which Greeks maintained with Italians changed considerably in time. Though membership in the community served their need for cultural and ethnic differentiation, it was flexible enough to allow for daily contact and communication with 'others'. It appears that the Italian army's defeat by the British (1941) favoured the appearance of more egalitarian relationships with Greeks: encouraged by the modification in the local hierarchy of power, the latter attempted to improve their social image by 'making their ascribed ethnic characteristics less burdensome' (Hannerz 1974: 63).

Such attempts were more successful among members of the second generation who were better qualified in terms of education and training: they graduated from Italian high schools and colleges, spoke the language fluently and were well acquainted with many Italians. Command over western skills and patterns of consumption was utilized as a tool in reinforcing their cultural basis and ethnic identity: they built houses in the wealthiest neighbourhoods of Asmara, eagerly admitted that 'not all Italians are fascist', developed new types of collaboration and social contact with them, and socialized in Italian clubs, on golf courses and on safaris. Undoubtedly, these activities attracted the approval of Italians who maintained public services and government departments even after the British occupation, but seemed to find it less meaningful to insist on the cultural cleavage between themselves and Greeks.

The establishment of interpersonal relationships with Italians was further manifested by intermarriage – a practice which was formerly unthinkable since both sides were preoccupied with cultural and social distinctions. One of the cases I came across is worth mentioning: six brothers and sisters were married to Italians in spite of their father's intense disagreement. Their affinal ties strengthened their social prestige, added to their negotiating power in many realms of local life and facilitated their departure during the war against Ethiopians.

To enhance the stereotypical attributes ascribed to them, younger Greeks made frequent use of criteria which were initially negated by their parents. For instance, they underlined their 'vital resemblances' with Italians – i.e. their endowment with the so-called Mediterranean temperament which allowed for an open expression of sentiments and feelings. Moreover, in referring to ex-colonists, they employed the term 'European', often associating 'European' descent with 'higher breed'. Their tendency to 'discover' similarities with the hegemonic tradition coexisted with an effort to dissociate themselves from all sorts of behaviour that might be thought of as demeaning other: hence, they emphasized their humanitarian principles and ability to 'start from scratch', as opposed to Italians' disinterest in natives' welfare and reliance on an impersonal administrative apparatus.

In the course of these revisions, Greeks were placed in an ambiguous position: on the one hand, they treasured their glorious national past while on the other, they no longer perceived Italians as a threatening group from which they had to distance themselves through delimiting distinctive characteristics. In dealing with this ambiguity, they aimed to enhance their ethnic identity: they realized that in order to confirm their cultural superiority and ability to adapt to social and economic crises – crucial signs of what they conceived as Greekness – they had to justify their choices with reference to the behaviour of the locally dominant group. By borrowing symbols from its members' lifestyle, they were able socially to interact with them and ensure a new basis of their status in the local society without reneging on their cultural heritage – as older migrants sometimes accused them of doing.

'Race and colour set people apart'

It thus comes as no surprise that social discriminations were far more prominent in the interaction between Greeks and Eritreans – and this is especially true for the first generation of migrants. Though they originally worked side by side in governmental projects, they did not always compete in the same labour market. The training of Eritreans was slow in transmitting those skills that would allow them to exploit new and demanding oppor-tunities. In contrast, Greeks did not only make significant commercial pro-gress, but also hired Eritreans as cooks or servants in their houses and labourers or technicians in their companies. Their expanding enterprises affected their views about the local population and motivated statements such as 'blacks can't do much on their own'.

The ties they created with Eritreans mirror the boundaries they set and the ways in which their stereotypes were activated: subtle as well as conspicuous aspects of behaviour signalled contempt, embarrassment and a wish to offer financial assistance but not personal services. Though they attended the feasts of their Eritrean labourers and servants, they did not actively participate in them. Neither did they return their invitations, learn their songs or adopt their dietary habits. Besides, they maintained that cultural distance between them was insuperable: 'it was hard for 'us' to be with 'them': they were dirty, ate with their hands... we avoided to take them by car for they walked bare-foot'.

The ways in which Greeks perceived and arranged their relationships with Eritreans also reflected distinctions based on colour: 'black and white' is, of course a prevalent mode of conceptualizing diversity in multi-ethnic societies and can underpin the foundations of local stratifi-cation systems (Phoenix 1988). Indeed, racial discrimination together with the power hierarchy it corresponded to, implied that members of different groups saw the division between themselves and others as simultaneously one of cultural identity and class. Greeks were repulsed by the conditions governing life in east Africa which surpassed what they had known until then. One may think here of the absence of drainage systems and the cohabitation of villagers and cattle in small huts. Such experiences combined with their wish to prepare the ground for a better future and urged them to draw a demarcating line between themselves and 'blacks' whose low standards of living were often interpreted as a product of innate incompetence.

Two final points should be made about the interaction between Greek migrants and Eritreans. Judging from the absence of traditions and monuments similar to what they had learned to value, they claimed that natives 'have no culture at all' and expressed surprise at customs which seemed 'barbarian' and inexplicable to them, such as the payment of brideprice. Besides, though the Eritrean population consisted of many tribes and corporate groupings some of which were wealthier and more progressive than others – e.g. the Muslim Jiberti – Greeks perceived them as culturally undifferentiated. This assumed homogeneity aimed to condemn natives to an 'inescapable fate' and contrasts starkly with the fact that in Greek culture, group membership and geographical origin are widely thought to attest to innate talents and capacities. It is also linked to the fact that they were more eager to accumulate information about those who were socially superior to them than about those who were inferior.

'Mixed marriages? No but ...'

It goes without saying that mixed marriages were out of the question for many years. The first migrants seem to have been almost categorical in that matter and were preoccupied with the practice of endogamy. It was in their interest to ward off incursions into their livelihood by outsiders: so long as Greeks held an intermediate position between the dominant and subordinate groups in Asmara they hardly, if ever, thought of marrying with either of them. To do so would have been taken as neglect of cultural norms, and as far as Eritreans were concerned, it might also have undermined plans to achieve higher standards of living. These points were explained to me in detail by an Eritrean woman married to a Greek merchant. Though she liked him from the start, she doubted the wisdom of her intention to marry him, fearing that she would have serious problems with her children's upbringing. Indeed, the couple suffered sanctions by both Greeks and Eritreans. The attitudes of the latter are understood better in view of their tendency to identify Greeks with Italians who 'exploited local resources with little in return'. As the woman confessed, her kin did not actually object to her love affair: what they disagreed with were marriage and the parenting of children – public social facts which could not be concealed. Social interaction then, had two sides which corresponded to two different dimensions of label- ling: one side is socially acceptable, while the other is frowned upon and should remain hidden.

As one might assume, there were no unions between Eritrean men and Greek women: bearing children to males of another cultural group was thought to 'betray the whole community'. By contrast, Greek men had less difficulty in expressing their admiration for 'native girls' beauty' and proposed to them: since in both Greek and Eritrean culture it is men who define the couple's status, their job and lifestyle made up for the women's social inferiority. What I found especially illuminating in this respect, concerns marriages between Greek men and *migades*, i.e. off- spring of marriages between Italians and Eritreans, whose identity was considered ambiguous. Though such unions were rather few, they give evidence of the extent to which Greek settlers' marital choices were conditioned by considerations of cultural proximity. Last but not least, the distinction between 'us' and 'them', invariably coloured Greeks' evaluations of intermarriage with natives. I was told that Eritreans were considered loyal and conscientious workers; they could be fully trusted with money and child care, and grasped whatever they were told at once. The emphasis on such qualities, however, provides an excellent basis for the establishment of unequal relationships rather than com- panionship. Their repercussions on the social ties between natives and Greeks are summarized well by an old Eritrean woman: 'Marriage? No, you [i.e. Greeks] never divided Asmara in two parts as Italians did, yet you never endeavoured to go beyond a certain point of intimacy with us...'

Religion and identity

Religion was a key factor in the process of identity construction. Greeks' devotion to *Orthodoxia* penetrated many levels of daily life: they fasted, received Holy Communion, donated money and clothes to the poor and aged members of the community, and exchanged sweets on religious holidays (a habit that prevailed among women). Despite the fact that until the 1950s the great majority of the Eritrean population were Christian Copts,[5] Greeks attended exclusively their own church which was financed by private savings and decorated with sacred items brought from their homeland. The restoration of familiar religious structures aimed to ascertain a meaningful world that would facilitate their adaptation to the new environment. It further contributed to a sense of social and symbolic autonomy which proved invaluable as a means of differentiating themselves from both non-Christian groups – Arabs, Indians or Jews – and other Christians – Armenian or Italian Catholics and Eritrean or Egyptian Copts.

Knowing the work of Christian missionaries in Africa, Greeks often claimed that Christianity was 'the best religion of all'. Nonetheless, they made explicit distinctions between Christian doctrines: Catholicism was considered quite remote from 'true human nature', while Orthodox doctrine endowed everyone with honesty, goodwill and hospitality. Interestingly enough, they referred to Eritreans' religiousness in two different ways: on the one hand, they saw it as 'very close' to their own faith, but on the other, it was evaluated as 'impure' because natives engaged in African customs involving magic and sorcery. Though none of the Greeks I met could recall an occasion on which magic was actually practised, they utilized such convictions with a straightforward intention: to point out that 'Greeks are better Christians than others'.

Though I have very little information about Greeks' relationships with Muslims, it appears that they had few or no relationships with them. At the root of this cleavage lay the more fundamental and historical opposition with Turks: especially the older generation identified Muslims with the 'worst enemy of the Greek nation' and were astonished to find out that Muslim villagers lived in peace with the rest of the population.

The 'reversal' of social interaction with Eritreans

Greeks' interaction with Eritreans changed considerably over time: many of them eventually expressed a great interest in Eritrean culture and concepts of time, sexual roles and leisure; many visited their homes and became acquainted with their kin, bought and delivered medicine in the countryside, praised their ethos and referred to them by their names rather than as 'blacks' or 'Africans'. This 'reversal' of Greeks' attitudes towards natives spread among the second generation because of two main factors. The first relates to the bonds established between natives and Europeans in colonial times (Eriksen 1991: 135): many Eritreans attended Italian and American colleges – some also went to the Greek primary school and later on to the University of Athens – and were employed in the public sector, mainly the administration or the military, or set up small enterprises to trade local products. The second factor is connected to Greeks' educational and economic qualifications. The effectiveness with which they responded to local opportunities (their wealth is easily discerned from photographs showing their beautiful houses, gardens, pieces of furniture etc.) had an important impact on the way in which they perceived themselves and others: it encowaged a sense of 'ethnic' superiority and allowed them to maintain a desirable status within the local society without having to obey rigid rules of preference and avoidance. Instead, they contributed actively to natives' welfare and took pride in demonstrating that Greeks were more broad-minded and humanist than the members of other ethnic groups. Hence, while Greeks were expected to observe a segregational ideology for the sake of their perceived cultural and ethnic identity, younger migrants imposed their own categories of social ascription and partly modified the nature of their social relationships with natives. The point at stake was no longer the commemoration of a glorious Greek history, nor was it used as a means of bridging past and present: they were far more concerned with their future and thus proceeded to negotiate their identity on the basis of multiple components.

Changing life prospects: Greeks settle in Athens

The Greek community in Asmara dispersed in the late 1970s when Eritrea fell under the control of Ethiopian occupation forces.[6] This led to various forms of persecution, and thousands of refugees fled to Sudan, OECD countries and the Middle East, while most Europeans abandoned the country, leaving their jobs and wealth behind.

The reinterpretation of Greekness
Once Greeks moved to a new environment, the criteria by which they defined themselves and others underwent dramatic changes. In the first place, they found it hard to cope with the consequences which the 'repatriation' process had forced on their lifestyle. Few of them had ever visited Greece in the past, and as a result of tax and state regulations they found it unprofitable to re-establish the companies they had run in Eritrea. In effect, they had to look for salaried employment. The loss of autonomy at work, the replacement of their detached houses with less comfortable apartments, and the disappointment they felt when they realized how little help they would receive from the Greek state, combined to augment their sense of uprootedness and predisposed them negatively towards their compatriots. Conversely, it appears that the response they received from other Greeks and even their relatives was not very friendly: their uncles and cousins, most of whom they had never met before, felt obliged to visit the newcomers once, but did not warmly invite them to their homes, fearing that they would be expected to offer financial or other assistance. Besides, they seemed to envy their past economic success and attempted to denigrate it by criticizing their skill in 'exploiting' natives. In their eyes, Greeks who had lived in Asmara had made 'easy money' in a country which provided the essential prerequisites, but lacked the cultural background of Greece.

To these reproaches, the newcomers responded in various ways. Some altogether avoided their kin, while others tried to remain on good terms with them. None, however, adopted an attitude of humility. Instead, they stressed the initiatives they had taken in circumstances where 'others would have died' and underlined their role in the development of the Eritrean economy. They also pointed out that Asmara was far ahead of Athens since the beginning of the century,[7] and they compared the anarchy of the Greek bureaucracy with the order, reliability and efficiency of the Italian and British administrative systems. Trying to define a world of their own, they overemphasized the cosmopolitan character of their former lives and the advantageous effects that living side by side with numerous groups had taken on their outlook and mental horizons. The way in which Greeks from Asmara perceived their compatriots is further thrown into relief by what I would refer to as 'careful impression management'. Thus, they often expressed their preference for each other's company or the company of Italian friends and affines, especially at feasts and gatherings where they tended to speak Italian or even Tigrai. The stories they now tell about Eritrea are not always accurate, but tend to exaggerate the harmony inherent in their relationships with other ethnic groups. There is no doubt, however, that they confirm the importance now accorded, among the returnees, to social interaction with different cultures as an indicator of both their democratic principles and their communicative experience.

Surprisingly, perhaps, most returnees do not feel themselves as forming part of the larger nation, nor do they praise their 'national' identity: instead, they denote the specificity of their personal history by referring to themselves as 'Africans'. To make up for the losses they have suffered, they conceptualize themselves as a 'minority' group which is qualified as such by distinct and 'superior' characteristics based on past rights and privileges: it is not 'them' who should be blamed for the difficulties they face after returning, but 'other' Greeks who cannot understand that they are entitled to special attention and treatment. Hence, although they no longer possess the luxuries they had in Eritrea, they still rely on intimate bonds which perpetuate their identification with their former location and relationships.

In praising the moral values of non-discriminatory and unprejudiced interaction, 'Africans' desire to prove their liberal principles as a product of multiethnic interaction in Eritrea. The use which they thus make of their past experiences mirrors more than a need to give meaning to their former life: it gives evidence of a motive to revise their past so as to enhance the claim that they are 'more Greek' than those who have not been required to maintain their cultural heritage in a hostile environment and to interact on good terms with numerous heterogeneous groups. Since these practices do not fade away with time but are carried on by their children, it is possible to say that they constitute key elements of the way in which they construct their new collective identity.

'Africans'' interaction with Eritreans in Athens

The process whereby appeal to the past helps repatriated groups to reconstruct their identity is documented by Hirschon in connection with Asia Minor refugees (Hirschon-Philippaki 1993). The findings here presented, however, add to our knowledge about the development of migrants' relationships with those who represent the host country, in this case Eritreans. 'Africans' have little to do with Eritrean refugees in Athens. Though they appreciate their honesty and have encouraged and subsidized their struggle for independence and self-determination, they rarely mix with them socially and tend to overlook the ties they retain with native families in Asmara. When listening to their conversations, it becomes clear that they share a claim to superiority vis-à-vis other Greeks, but do not use relationships with Eritreans in Greece as a means of defining their identity. Through a 'shared amnesia' (Gellner 1987: 6), 'Africans' 'forget' that they have lived among other Eritrean people for many decades, and they contrast their European qualities to the lower backgrounds ascribed to 'Southerners'. More often then not, they regard African Eritreans in Greece as cheap manpower to fill in the lowest occupational categories and worry about the impact that contacts with socially inferiors might have on their status.

This emphasis on 'Europeaness' differs from the value they once assigned to their cultural similarities with Italians: it is now employed as a means of distinction, rather than as an identification with the stereo-typical characteristics of another ethnic group. In either case, however, one can easily see that it is an admiration of 'western' modes of beha-viour which sets the terms under which claim to the Greek classical heritage is defended (Herzfeld 1982: 75ff).

A final word about the interplay between processes of identification and processes of social interaction (Barth 1969: 15-16) must consider those 'Africans' who have married Eritrean women. These people per-ceive Greekness as a concept which not only goes beyond spatial boundaries, but also covers the offspring of mixed marriages. As was the case in Asmara, such unions continue to face negative sanctions, and 'mixed' couples are often avoided by both spouses' kin and face great difficulties in expanding their social networks. To overcome these restrictions, Eritrean women do their best to find acceptance among their husbands' relatives: they try to 'be friendly with them', prepare Greek dishes, attend Orthodox Church services, and emulate other markers of Greekness. In so doing, they aim to prepare a better future for their children who, considered 'black', confront serious problems at school. In addition to aspects of racism manifest in school text books, these children are subject to ridicule by their classmates. I recall here but one incident of a little girl returning from school in tears: some of her classmates had said that all Africans were cannibals. Tellingly, when the Director of the school refused to intervene, her father lost his composure and slapped him in the face.

Concluding remarks

This paper has addressed the subjective experience of ethnic identity, its variations and manipulations in time and space, and the link of that experience to social interaction. I have argued that identity construction is a dialectic precipitate of contradictory elements: old and new, national and local, personal and communal. Though it is culturally bounded, it is neither stable nor fixed: it is ephemeral, dynamic and negotiable; is generated in apparently distorted, and certainly tortuous, ways; and varies according to the social and historical setting as well as the position of those who interact. 'Ethnic' claims can thus be understood as elaborations of social and political claims built upon perceived commonalities within the putative group and upon categorical differences from 'others'.

The data clearly show that 'Africans' do not organize their lives and relationships in terms of 'ethnic' distinctions. Self-presentation requires skills, and it is subject to strategic manipulations that involve differences in culture, religion, and 'race', as well as access to social and economic power. Having been an intermediary group in a colonial situation which stressed reified 'cultural' and 'ethnic' boundaries, and having turned into a 'minority' in their own country, 'African' Greeks have had to negotiate their identity in multiple ways. One of these was the provision of goods and services that were locally valued; another, the adoption of attributes of the hegemonic tradition and the dissociation from people whom they regarded as inferior. Clearly, interrelating with 'others' served to constitute an arena in which stereotypical qualities could be questioned, as well as revalidated.

Identity manipulation is not, of course, an easy or, for that matter, a voluntarist pursuit. Its concrete components cannot be fully dissimulated, and social action remains circumscribed by the structural framework, the assignment of statuses and roles, and a host of other factors. Nonetheless, such constraints are relevant, rather than determinative. Hence, what is considered 'Greek' becomes a matter of contestation in the context of relationships with perceived cultural groups, as well as members of the group one identifies with. Greekness further reflects the varying experiences of successive generations: in this case, it was perceived in opposing ways by two generations of settlers who made use of the resources available to them in terms of social prestige and/or material rewards. In effect, pioneer migrants perceived their identity as a fragile and ambiguous element that had to be protected from foreign elements and should be acknowledged by those who made decisions. In contrast, younger migrants saw it as a quality of collective high status that need not fear interaction with other categorical groups.

Though 'schizophrenic' at first sight, the oppositions observed in the process of identity construction do make sense once they are placed within the context that defined 'Africans'' lives at specific historical junctions. In Asmara, they were 'European' at work, 'Greek' in their leisure time; obliging to the colonial power and condescending to those who were colonized; in their country of origin, however, where power relations and structural settings were altogether transformed, they felt 'African' and kept distance from both their compatriots and refugee Eritreans. Their experiences challenge a view prevalent in studies of ethnicity in urban situations, namely that inter-ethnic ties impede the development of class solidarity (Cohen 1969; Hannerz 1974). Neither the establishment of social ties with colonists, nor the denial of parochial allegiances and the existence of social inequalities within the

Greek community in Asmara, prevented Greeks from belonging to one or the other social class as it was expressed in terms of education, material wealth, place of residence, lifestyle or social relationships. Ethnic identity, then, is a product of choices, negotiations and debate, and it has currency within a specific discourse. What people 'are' is determined within the frame of concrete social behaviours and relationships, justifications and symbols, the meanings of which are historically and situationally defined.

Notes

1. Ethnic identity has been defined both as a structural concept, an abstract by means of which analysts explain the conduct of actors (Cohen and Middleton 1970) and as a cultural or cognitive category based on the significance people attribute to perceptible cultural distinctions (Mitchell 1974: 31).

2. The definition of identity must imply 'condensation of past events in the present', since successive changes in lifestyle are filtered through current belief systems and positions. Turner puts this emphatically: it is structurally indifferent whether the past is real or not. What matters is the meaning of living relations and experiences (Turner 1986: 33-44).

3. This project is subsidized by the National Centre for Social Research and UNESCO.

4. During 1987-89, almost 6,000 Eritreans entered Greece but have since then moved to Canada and the U.S.A. In 1993, there are little more than 300 of them living in Athens.

5. In 1943, the population of Asmara counted some 172,000 Copts, 2,000 Catholics, 32,000 Muslims and 3,000 Protestants (Longrigg 1945, Appendix C).

6. The U.N. created the Eritrean Ethiopian Federation against the expressed will of the Eritrean people who resisted the annexation of the country (1950) and gradually resorted to armed struggle in 1961 (Commission for Eritrean Refugee Affairs 1989).

7. Asmara was indeed one of the leading African cities with 40,000 Europeans and 60,000 native inhabitants (Longrigg 1950: 138).

References

Barth, F.
  1969   *Ethnic Groups and Boundaries: The Social Organization of Cultural Difference*. London: Allen & Unwin.
Berreman, G.
  1972   Social Categories and Social Interaction in Urban India. *American Anthropologist* 74, 3: 567-586.
Chapman, M., McDonald M. et al.
  1989   Introduction to Tonkin et al. (eds.) 1989, pp. 1-21.
Cohen, A. (ed.)
  1974   *Urban Ethnicity*. London: Tavistock.
Cohen, A.
  1985   *The Symbolic Construction of Community*. London: Tavistock.
Cohen, R. and J. Middleton
  1970   Introduction. In: R. Cohen, J. Middleton (eds.), *From Tribe to Nation in Africa: Studies in Incorporation Processes*. London: Routledge & Kegan Paul, pp. 1-34.
Cole, J.
  1977   Anthropology Comes Part Way Home. *Annual Review of Anthropology* 6.
Commission for Eritrean Refugee Affairs
  1989   *The Eritrean Refugee Problem: Issues and Challenges*. London: CERA.
Epstein, A.
  1978   *Ethos and Identity*. London: Tavistock.
Eriksen, T.
  1991   The Cultural Contexts of Ethnic Differences. *Man* 26, 1: 127-144.
Gellner, E.
  1987   *Culture, Identity and Politics*. Cambridge: Cambridge University Press.
Goffman, E.
  1958   *The Presentation of Self in Everyday Life*. Edinburgh: University of Edinburgh, Monograph no. 2.
Hannerz, U.
  1974   Ethnicity and Opportunity in Urban America. In: Cohen (ed.). pp. 37-76.
Herzfeld, M.
  1982   *Ours Once More. Folklore, Ideology and the Making of Modern Greece*. Austin, Tx.: University of Texas Press.

Hirschon-Philippaki, R.
  1983   Mnimi kai Tautotita. Oi Mikrasiates Prosfyges tis Kokkinias. In: E. Papata-
         xiarchis and Th. Paradellis (eds.) *Anthropologia kai Parelthon*. Athens:
         Alexandreia, pp. 327-356.

Hobsbawn, E. and T. Ranger
  1983   *The Invention of Tradition*. Cambridge: Cambridge University Press.

Just, R.
  1989   Triumph of the Ethnos. In: Tonkin et al. (eds.), pp. 71-88.

Longrigg, S.
  1945   *A Short History of Eritrea*. Oxford: Clarendon Press.

McDonald, M.
  1986   Celtic Ethnic Kinship and the Problems of Being English. *Current Anthro-
         pology* 27, 4: 333-341.

Mitchell, J.
  1974   Perceptions of Ethnicity and Ethnic Behaviour. In: Cohen (ed.), pp. 1-35.

Papamichael, M.
  1950   *O Ana tin Afriki Ellinismos*. Alexandreia: Anatoli.

Petronoti, M.
  1992   The Analysis of Life Histories as a Methodological Tool in Anthropological
         Research. In: D. Trakas, E. Sanz (eds.), *Studying Childhood and Medicine
         Use. A Multidisciplinary Approach*. Athens: ZHTA Medical Publications,
         pp. 67-77.

Phoenix, A.
  1988   Narrow Definitions of Culture. The Case of Early Motherhood. In: S. West-
         wood and P. Bhachu (eds.), *Enterprising Women. Ethnicity, Economy and
         Gender Relations*. London: Routledge, pp. 152-176.

Tonkin, E., McDonald, M. and Chapman, M. (eds.)
  1989   *History and Ethnicity*. ASA Monographs 27, London: Routledge.

Triantafyllou, K.
  1972   *Pangosmios Ellinodiktis*. Athens: Patrai.

Turner, V.
  1986   Dewey, Dilthey and Drama. An Essay in the Anthropology of Experience.
         In: V. Turner, E. Bruner (eds.), *The Anthropology of Experience*. Urbana and
         Chicago: University of Illinois Press, pp. 33-44.

Notes on contributors

Madawi Al-Rasheed studied Social Anthropology at the University of Cambridge and was a Prize Research Fellow at Nuffield College, Oxford. Currently, she is a lecturer at the Institute of Social and Cultural Anthropology, Oxford University. Her first research was related to tribes, dynasties, and the state in the Arabian Peninsula. More recently, she conducted fieldwork among Arab communities in London, in particular among Iraqi exiled groups. Her publications include *Politics in an Arabian Oasis* (London: I.B. Taurus 1991). She is currently preparing a monograph on Assyrian Christians. From September 1995, she will be lecturer in Social Anthropology at King's College, London University.

Gerd Baumann studied Social Anthropology at the Queen's University of Belfast and the University of Oxford where he held a Junior Research Fellowship at Wolfson College. After ten years' research on the Sudan, he moved to Brunel The University of West London, and began seven years' fieldwork among the inhabitants of Southall, one of London's most populous multi-ethnic areas. Since 1993, he holds a Readership at the Research Centre Religion and Society, University of Amsterdam. His publications include *The Written Word: Literacy in Transition* (Oxford: Clarendon Press 1986), *National Integration and Local Integrity: The Miri of the Nuba Mountains in the Sudan* (Oxford: Clarendon Press 1987) and, currently in press, *Contesting Culture: Discourses of Identity in Multi-Ethnic London* (Cambridge University Press 1996).

Flip Lindo studied Sociology and Social Anthropology at the University of Amsterdam before conducting fieldwork in Macedonian Greece and, subsequently, research among Greek and other Mediterranean migrants in the Netherlands. Currently working at the University of Utrecht and under the auspices of the Netherlands Organization for Scientific Research, he is about to complete a comparative study on the educational achievement of Iberian and Turkish post-migration youth in Holland. His publications include analyses of power relations on the national and village level in Greece, as well as the edited collection *Vier jaar na de Nota: balans van het minderhedenbeleid* (Utrecht: Nederlands Centrum Buitenlanders 1988) and, with T. Pennings, *Jeugd met toekomst. De leefsituatie van Portugese, Spaanse en Joegoslavische jongeren in Nederland* (Amsterdam: Het Spinhuis 1992).

Mies van Niekerk studied Social Anthropology at the University of Amsterdam and has conducted research among Surinamese girls in the Netherlands, participated in a project on inter-ethnic relations in a post-war urban neighbourhood of Haarlem, and published a study of the position of old-age immigrants. She is currently engaged in research on the role of ethnic differences in social mobility of Surinamese Creoles and Hindustanis residents in the Netherlands. Her publications include *De tijd zal spreken. Antilliaanse en Turkse ouderen in Nederland* (Amsterdam: 't Spinhuis 1990), *Kansarmoede. Reacties van allochtonen op achterstand*. (Amsterdam: 't Spinhuis 1993).

Marina Petronoti studied Sociology at Deree College, Athens, and Social Anthropology at Pantheion University, Athens, and the University of Kent at Canterbury. She has conducted fieldwork in both rural and urban areas of Greece, focusing on marital prestation, customary law, family organization, and contemporary modes of entrepreneurship. Currently working at the National Centre of Social Research, Athens, she is in charge of a UNESCO research project on ethnic minorities in Greece. Her publications include the recent monograph *Networks of Social Relationships: Their Interaction with Processes of Occupational Mobility* (Athens: National Centre of Social Research 1995).

Thijl Sunier studied Cultural Anthropology at the Universities of Utrecht and Amsterdam, participated in research on inter-ethnic relations a post-war neighbourhood of Haarlem, and conducted research among Turkish youth in the Netherlands. Currently a research fellow and lecturer at the Free University, Amsterdam, he is engaged in research on Turkish Muslim organizations in the Netherlands. His publications include numerous articles on Muslims in Europe, Islam and politics in Turkey and Central Asia, the monograph *Bekende Vreemden. Turken, Surinamers en Nederlanders in een naoorlogse wijk* (Amsterdam: 't Spinhuis 1989), and the collection *Macht, Mobilisatie en Moskee* (Baarn: Ambo 1991).

Marlene de Vries studied Sociology at the Universities of Amsterdam and Leiden. In cooperation with the Ministry of Welfare, she conducted research on the position of post-migration youth in education and the labour market, and later her doctoral fieldwork among Turkish young women in Amsterdam. Currently a member of the Institute for Migration and Ethnic Studies at the University of Amsterdam, she is at present engaged in research among Dutch Eurasians, which focuses on the intergenerational transmission of norms and values and its role in ethnic processes. Her publications include *Waar komen zij terecht? De positie van jeugdige allochtonen in het onderwijs en op de arbeidsmarkt* (The Hague: ACOM / Ministry of CRM 1981), *Ogen in je Rug. Turkse meisjes en jonge vrouwen in Nederland* (Alphen aan de Rijn: Samson 1987), and *Roddel nader beschouwd* (Leiden: COMT 1990).

Lale Yalçın-Heckmann studied Sociology at the Boğazici University, Istanbul, and social anthropology at the London School of Economics. Having completed her doctoral research on Kurdish tribes and kinship in southern Turkey, she took up a teaching appointment at the Middle East Technical University in Ankara before moving to Germany. From 1988, she has been conducting research on Muslims and Turks in Germany. Currently, Dr. Yalçin-Heckmann is a research fellow at the Chair of Turkish Studies of the University of Bamberg. Her publications include numerous articles on Kurdish ethnography and ethnicity, the monograph *Tribe and Kinship among the Kurds* (Frankfurt: Peter Lang 1991), and extensive work on Islam and Turks in Germany and Europe.